OLD MEN BICYCLING ACROSS AMERICA

A JOURNEY BEYOND OLD AGE

FROSTY WOOLDRIDGE

authorHOUSE®

AuthorHouse™
1663 Liberty Drive
Bloomington, IN 47403
www.authorhouse.com
Phone: 1 (800) 839-8640

Published by AuthorHouse 12/19/2018

ISBN: 978-1-5462-7142-0 (sc)
ISBN: 978-1-5462-7141-3 (e)

Library of Congress Control Number: 2018914773

To

Sandi Lynn-Wooldridge, the love of my life, for her high energy, her humor, her sense of balance, her well-being, her dancing, and her infectious joy for life. She always brings a smile to my heart, mind and soul when we sit by a campfire somewhere in the world. I'm thankful she chose me to be her partner on the dance floor of life.

Your Life, Your Adventure, Your Journey

No matter how long your bicycle tour, no matter how many miles, no matter how many campfires and no matter how many amazing moments you experienced—your journey ultimately comes to an end. It might be a coast-to-coast, border-to-border or continent-to-continent, but like Thomas Stevens' first bicycle journey around the world from 1884 to 1886—you finally come to the finality of your expedition.

Captain Jean Luc Picard of the Starship Enterprise said it best, "Someone once told me that time was a predator that stalks us all our lives. I rather believe that time is a companion that goes with us on a journey. It reminds us to cherish each moment, because it will never come again. What we leave behind is not as important as how we lived."

Therefore, in this life, relish the highs, endure the lows and savor the in-between times. Pedal into those sunrises that light the sky with promise. Savor those elegant sunsets with their exclamation point to a glorious day on your bicycle. Remember the good, bad and ugly moments. Stand tall that you possessed the courage to explore the world on your iron steed. It carried you into your dreams where you traveled into those epic moments of wonder, awe and majesty.

Contents

Introduction

As baby boomers back in the days of our youth, we pedaled a bicycle on a paper route, off to school and/or pedaled with a bunch of friends onto backroads, into the woods or just screwed around on a city block.

Riding a bicycle provided fun, freedom and a sense of elation for our spirits. For the most part, we took it for granted. It didn't occur to us that a piece of steel, propelled by a chain drive, navigated by handlebars, and complimented with two rubber tires wrapped around metal rims—could carry us around the world.

As kids, we clipped playing cards to our spokes to make noise as if we rode a high-powered bike. We raced each other, cracked wheelies and escaped neighborhood dogs. Along the way, we crashed, tore our pants and skinned our knees.

Somehow, without helmets on our heads, we survived our childhoods. Not without a few chipped teeth, broken bones and bruised muscles!

As time passed, we graduated from high school only to buy a car or motorcycle. Millions of Schwinn bikes hung from the rafters of parents' garages. Some teens left for college, where they rode their bikes to class. But, after four years, they graduated into real life with jobs, cars and marriage.

Their bicycles found new rafters in the garage with plenty of dust dulling the finish over the years.

As for this cyclist, I remember my paper route days back in the 1960's. At first, I walked my 80-customer route. It burned a lot of time. I asked my dad if he would buy me a bicycle.

"If you want a bike," he said. "You earn it. Save up your paper route money and buy it on lay-away."

After four months, I plunked down $60.00 for a fat tire Schwinn Wasp. I added some baskets on the front and rear. It resembled a beast of burden.

With that bike, I sailed through my route. I threw a folded paper at the door and watched it break open, ready to read. I saw lots of deer, rabbits, turkeys and skunks in the early morning light. Birds chirped from the branches and waves of geese filled the skies during the autumn migrations. And those sunrises, well, they filled me with visual wonderment of the creativity of Mother Nature.

Of course, dogs found me as easy prey. They chased me, snapped at me, and tore pieces out of my trousers.

After my route, a hot shower and Wheaties with sliced bananas finished my morning routine. I pedaled off to school. You might say I enjoyed a great childhood. I loved that Schwinn Wasp. It gave me freedom and money. I bought an RCA transistor radio. The first song I remember: "Hound Dog" by Elvis Presley.

After high school, I rode to classes every day through my college years. During the last week of finals of my senior year, someone stole it. I cried at the loss of my friend. However, life called, and I moved forward to a teaching job in Colorado.

In the case of this cyclist and many others out of the 60's, the new high-speed Schwinn Continental with 10 gears, offered a whole new perspective in bicycle travel. I cranked up mountain passes with ease. I flat-out hauled ass on the flats with a flip of the lever.

A friend and I raced each other to work daily. We awoke early to bicycle eastbound for 24 miles to work at District 27-J on the arid plains in Brighton, Colorado. I taught math and science. We pedaled into glorious sunrises that sprayed the heavens with chameleon clouds and majestic thunderheads. Once at work, we showered and started our day. After work, we cranked west toward the mountains with stunning sunsets expanding the skies with a rainbow of colors. At that point, as a young man in my twenties, I felt the wonder of my bike, yet, I took it all for granted. I pedaled for transportation, not adventure.

On the Edge of Wonder

By 1974, I rode my CB 750 Honda motorcycle to Alaska. After crossing the Arctic Circle, I met two guys on bicycles stopped along the gravel road. I said, "What are you two doing up here on the Dalton Highway on bicycles?"

"We rode from San Diego, California to reach the Arctic Circle," one said.

I said, "A motorcycle will get you there faster and easier."

"Yeah," he said. "But all you do is turn the throttle and watch the scenery go by at 60 miles per hour. You miss most of it in one big blur. At 12 mph, the landscape etches memories into your thighs. You live on the edge of wonder every mile."

"On the edge of wonder," I muttered.

"Yup," he said. "On a bicycle tour, you become the adventure."

As I throttled away from those two guys, I ruminated about his comment, "on the edge of wonder" for several days. That single comment played on my mind for the next week. I throttled my motorcycle across the Alaskan wilderness, but in that one single comment with two guys exploring on bicycles, my life changed.

Back at school that autumn, I spoke with my riding buddy.

"Ward," I said. "What do you think of me bicycling coast-to-coast next year, Los Angeles to Jekyll Island, Georgia on the Atlantic?"

"Wish I could go with you," he said. "But my wife won't let me. Heck, you're single, so do it. It will transform you. It will be a thousand times more fun than our morning rides."

"Well, it sounds pretty crazy, but that touring cyclist in Alaska said that I would live on the 'edge of wonder' for the entire journey," I said.

"I've done week-long tours," Ward said. "That pretty much sums it up."

Coast to Coast

That next spring of 1975, I announced that I planned to bicycle coast-to-coast across America.

"You're crazy," said several colleagues. "You could get run over out there with the drunks or someone swatting their kids instead of keeping their eyes on the road."

Nonetheless, I figured if those two guys could pedal their butts up to Alaska, I could pedal 3,000 miles across America.

"I'm going," I said.

Perhaps I should have paused when I couldn't get anyone else to accompany me on that first bicycle adventure.

"You're nuts, man," buddies told me.

Nonetheless, I bought a bike billed as a 'touring bicycle' with racks, panniers, drop bars and mountain gearing.

For equipment, I carried a one-burner stove, pot and utensils. I bought rain gear, shorts and shanked shoes to protect my feet from being crushed with constant pedaling. I ordered an excellent helmet. I carried three water bottles, and extra underwear. For the most part, I didn't possess any idea about the perils of bicycle touring. Remember the adage, "You'll learn the hard way."

In June, I took a train out to Los Angeles. Several days later, I dipped the back tire of my steel-grey Miyata Gran Touring bike into the Pacific Ocean on Manhattan Beach. On the back of my rear pack, I displayed a sign, "Coast to Coast."

"That should get a little attention," I muttered to myself.

After pushing the bike through 100 yards of sand and plenty of strange people staring at me, I reached the pavement. I hopped onto the bike for a ride through the gridlocked Los Angeles traffic. Almost accidently, I pointed my left hand down to the ground and then, pointed it eastward, like Ward Bond in the TV series of the 60's, "Wagon Train", and said, "Forward, Ho!"

After two days of dodging LA traffic and inhaling copious amounts of smog, I reached the Mojave Desert heading toward the Colorado River and Arizona.

A New Understanding of Hunger

Sitting by a campfire one night, I looked up at the stars to see the Big Dipper, Orion and Aquarius. Shooting stars sliced through the ink-black night sky above me. The North Star twinkled into my eyes. I stirred my Dinty Moore vegetable stew while dipping bagels into the broth. For some reason, it tasted better than anything I had ever eaten before.

While devouring vegetable stew, peanuts, bagels, tomatoes, avocados, apples, peaches and just about everything else I could get my hands on, I felt a warm sense of happiness overwhelm me. The starlight gleamed off my bike metal. My tent and sleeping bag awaited me. In the distance, a coyote howled in the bush. Not to be outdone, a Great Horned Owl hooted through the night air with a sense of curiosity about this strange being on a bicycle who pitched a tent and built a campfire.

"Damn!" I said to myself. "This is cool stuff. I almost feel like I'm dreaming, but I'm awake and sitting here in the middle of my dream as I stare into the embers of this campfire. If I'm living on the edge of wonder, this bicycle touring, well, it's pretty cool."

That night transformed me into a long-distance touring bicycle traveler. Since then, I bicycled 14 times across the United States coast-to-coast and/or Canada to Mexico. I've bicycled and camped across six continents, including parts of Antarctica. It's been one hell of an extraordinary journey of animals, people, amazing sights and epic moments. One of my books encompasses those amazing moments, animals and people: **Around the World on a Bicycle—Tire Tracks for Your Imagination**.

And today, I'm 72 years of age. I don't take anything for granted anymore. Every day I am alive and healthy proves a bonus. I hang with guys who are gray-haired, gray-bearded, bald and struggling with high blood pressure. They face enlarged prostate glands, cancer and knee-hip replacements. Some chose heart by-pass surgery. One friend suffers from Alzheimer's disease. I attended three funerals in the spring before this ride across America. It's a fact: getting old ain't for sissies.

Journey Beyond Old Age

If you like to pedal a bicycle or you once loved to ride a bike, this book may inspire you. If you're facing old age or standing in the middle of it somewhere between 60 and 80, you're looking out a window that narrows with each daybreak. With that in mind, I invited a bunch of my 65 to 70-year-old friends to accompany me on the Northern Tier of a coast-to-coast bicycle ride across the United States. It started in Astoria, Oregon and ended in Bar Harbor, Maine. It spanned 4,300 miles.

If this book ignites your imagination, the last three chapters instruct you in everything you need to know on how to start your own bicycle adventure across America.

You're invited to share this journey in words, songs, people and animals. It's the stuff of life. While you're alive on this planet, let my friends show you how to charge toward living. Life provides you with this unique moment of adventure.

"If the roar of a wave crashes beyond your campsite, you might call that adventure. When coyotes howl outside your tent—that may be adventure. While you're sweating like a horse in a climb over a 12,000-foot pass, that's adventure. When a howling headwind presses your lips against your teeth, you're facing a mighty adventure. If you're pushing through a howling rainstorm, you're soaked in adventure. But that's not what makes an adventure. It's your willingness to struggle through it, to present yourself at the doorstep of Nature. That creates the experience. No more greater joy can come from life than to live inside the 'moment' of an adventure. It may be a momentary 'high', a stranger that changes your life, an animal that delights you or frightens you, a struggle where you triumphed, or even failed, yet you braved the challenge. Those moments present you uncommon experiences that give your life eternal expectation. That's adventure!" Frosty Wooldridge

THE CHARACTERS WHO
MAKE UP A JOURNEY

On this journey, I invited a bunch of old farts from 65 to 72. Each brought his unique life story to the campfire. Each brought a lifetime of experiences. Two friends never toured before. Two enjoyed veteran tours across Europe and the USA. Two I met while touring across America. One I met when my wife's girlfriend introduced me to her boyfriend. He loved cycling, but never ventured past a day ride.

Before the tour, I wrote out a few rules for the tour as to safety, getting along and best tires to buy. I suggested flags and blinkers. I sent out packing lists. I did everything I could do to make for a smooth and friendly ride. However, no matter what I did, the trip would create its own personality. The great author John Steinbeck stated it best in his book, **Travels with Charley: In Search of America.**

"Once a journey is designed, equipped, and put in process, a new factor enters and takes over. A trip, a safari, an exploration, is an entity, different from all other journeys. It has personality, temperament, individuality, uniqueness. A journey is a person in itself; no two are alike. And all plans, safeguards, policing, and coercion are fruitless. We find after years of struggle that we do not take a trip; a trip takes us. Tour masters, schedules, reservations, brass-bound and inevitable, dash themselves to wreckage on the personality of the trip. Only when this is recognized can the blown-in-the glass bum relax and go along with it. Only then do the frustrations fall away. In this a journey is like marriage. The certain way to be wrong is to think you control it."

Like Steinbeck said, "...we don't take a trip; a trip takes us."

That's what happened on this journey: old men carry lots of baggage, some anger issues such as divorces, various personal disappointments, lots of bias and endless opinions. All of those factors boiled to the surface whether positive or negative. Each personality presented all of us with opportunities for laughter, anger, singing, frustration and fellowship. At the same time, one fellow vented on his fellow cyclists for reasons beyond our understanding. Some guys make it easy to get along and others try to bait you, get your goat and outright insult you. We dealt with such events with wisdom and integrity.

All in all, we enjoyed a magnificent ride.

NORTHERN TIER ACROSS AMERICA

Known as the Northern Tier bicycle route across America, it boasts the most mileage at 4,310 miles. It starts in Astoria, Oregon to hug the border with Canada and ends up in Bar Harbor, Maine. More uniquely, it follows the famous "Lewis & Clark Trail" for 1,500 miles to Bismarck, North Dakota.

After the Louisiana Purchase, President Thomas Jefferson, from 1804-1806, commissioned Lewis & Clark, along with 33 men, to explore the vast unknown expanse to find a water passage route to the Pacific. They started in St. Louis, Missouri and headed up the Missouri River.

We visited Fort Clatsop where they wintered over in 1805 after reaching the Pacific Ocean. They built the fort within two weeks. It featured a water source, plenty of game and access to the Pacific Ocean. Dreadfully, according to Sergeant Ordway's journal, out of three months, it rained every day but 12, and the sun shined only six days total out of those 12 days. In other words, they lived a miserable existence with bed bugs, fleas, mosquitos, cold temperatures, wet weather, and cut off from the world.

Their route carried us along the mighty Columbia River, up and through the Cascade Mountains and across the Northern Great Plains. We camped where those 33 men camped. We pedaled into the Columbia River Gorge out of Troutdale, Oregon. It remains much the same today with wilderness thicker than hair on a dog. After the leaving the Columbia River, we followed the Clearwater River and on to Lolo Pass at 5,233 feet.

We rode from there into Great Falls, Montana and on across the plains to Bismarck, North Dakota. We continued on toward Duluth, Minnesota to Ashland, Wisconsin and on to Marquette, Michigan. We crossed the Mackinaw Bridge to lower Michigan to Port Huron where we crossed into Canada to reach Niagara Falls.

We continued east into the Adirondack Mountains of New York and into Vermont, New Hampshire and on to Bar Harbor, Maine. If you want a visual or hard copy map of the ride, you may visit AdventureCycling.org to obtain a map of the "Northern Tier" coast-to-coast across America. It gives you exact route numbers, campgrounds, amenities and much more.

At the Atlantic Ocean, we threw up our hands for a triumphant finish to a remarkable journey across America.

Theme for the ride: **"Keep pedaling because if you stop, old age catches up quickly."**

Aches and Pains of Old Age

If you think it's easy riding a bicycle past the age of 70, think again. You've got to deal with bad knees, failing hips, overweight issues and high blood pressure. You face circulation problems, joint issues, sore feet, and aches and pains in places you never knew existed. Your hands grow numb from pressure on the bars while your elbows and shoulders take a constant pounding from the road.

Additionally, we all sported gray hair and beards, or bald heads. There's nothing sexy about wrinkles, age spots, dark moles and pot bellies. Our teeth: not as white as in our youths. Skin sagging? Plenty in this group.

When we looked at ourselves in the mirror, the question jumped out, "How in the hell did I get this old this fast?"

Guess what? There's nothing you can do about it.

While I am lean and in great condition, I suffer from high blood pressure. My dad died of a heart attack at 46. My brother died at 50 of the same. My other brother suffered a stroke at 55. Presently, I follow **The Sinatra Solution** to lower my blood pressure via nutrients. I keep a steady 120/80 most days. You may find that book on Amazon.

Another thing that bugs me about getting old: I can't remember things that happened recently. While speaking, I can't find the right words to fit into a sentence. I "search" through my brain to find the word, but if I can't find it, I use another word. It's highly frustrating. It appears to be a slow, age-related cognitive decline, which hits most of us as we age. I take coconut oil and PS (phosphatidylserine) to keep as mentally sharp as possible. I'm not looking forward to what it will do to my brain when I reach 80, which, by the way, will arrive in a blink of time.

Additionally, three years ago, my right knee suffered breakdown from an old racquetball injury that kept getting worse. After the 2016 cross country ride, I figured my bicycle days might come to an end. Back in Denver, I heard about "Stem Cell Therapy." I watched Dr. Michael Cantor on "Ted Talks" give his presentation on the benefits over steel knee replacement. I booked an appointment the next week. After taking X-rays, they said my knee would respond with 99 percent healing.

"Your knee will be as good as new," Dr. Cantor said.

"Let's do it," I said.

He extracted marrow out of my bones and spun my blood into "platelet rich plasma." He reinjected the stem cells with my "super blood" back into my knee. Within the next 12 months, my knee healed to the point that I jumped back into the bumps for skiing. I still curried concern over the knee making a 4,300-mile bike trip. I trained to get my knee ready for such arduous pedaling. After two weeks and many mountain passes, my knee performed like a teenager. I pedaled 100-mile days or 50-mile days with no pain or freeze-up.

One of my friends on this ride sported 40 pounds of excess weight. He hated being fat. When he wore skin tight riding nylons and jerseys, that big pot belly stuck out like a sore thumb. His father died of a heart attack at 62, so he rode a delicate line between life and death. He tried to become a vegetarian like me, but he fell back into his voracious appetite and beer habits.

There's something to be said about, "eat, drink and be happy, for tomorrow you die." If you're enjoying your life with all your vices, it's your life, and you get to live it at your pleasure.

Another friend on this ride faced high cholesterol which could give him a stroke or heart attack on a mountain pass. For him, he might eat less red meat and dairy products, but, again, there's something to be said like Frank Sinatra, "I did it my way."

Finally, I explained that a laissez-fair attitude toward each other's bad habits would go a long way for group tranquility.

In the end, we're all here for a short time on this planet, so each of us gets to choose to make it a good time as we define it.

SPECTACULAR MOMENTS
WHILE ON TOUR

"The fear of death follows from the fear of life. A man who lives fully is prepared to die at any time." ~ *Mark Twain*

On my first bike trip to Alaska as a young adventure-seeker at 28, I woke up in my tent on the Russian River of the Kenai Peninsula hearing a "Grumph, grumph, emph" outside my tent. The Russian River enjoys fame not only for its salmon fishing, but also, its 1,000-pound grizzly bears. They visit the river to feed on millions of salmon racing for the spawning grounds.

I shot upright with a chill ripping down my spine. My brother Rex slept in his tent about 10 feet from mine. All night, I swatted no-see-ums, a tiny biting fly, but the bear posed greater danger. I opened my front flap to see an enormous grizzly looking right at me, not four feet away. As the breeze shifted, I smelled the worst case of halitosis in my life. He stunk worse than a barnyard.

He looked at me and I looked at him. My heart jumped out of my chest from beating so fast. My mouth dried up like a cotton ball in the desert. I coward with the strangest feeling of my short life! That bear could kill me in minutes. I wouldn't stand a chance.

Within 15 seconds, he ambled around the side of my tent. As he passed by the sidewalls, he rubbed his muzzle and drooled across the bright orange nylon. The sun shone through the tent to accent the drool-line about three feet long. Seconds later, he grunted some more and started digging at the corner of my tent. I looked back to see his claws rip through the nylon and hit the blue plastic flooring.

My eyes grew wide as I stared at the four-inch claws cutting through my tent. Seconds later, he withdrew them. He walked around my tent to walk right back in front of me. A moment later, he turned toward the Russian River to grab a mouthful of fresh salmon.

My brother Rex said, "Are we gonna' live or die? What's the verdict, bro?"

"Could go either way if he doesn't catch any fish," I said. "I think I just stared death in the face."

Like everything in life, random chance may kill you, let you live or hurt you—depending on the circumstances. That morning, which remains vividly with me to this day, could have turned out ugly. We could have been written up in the Anchorage morning newspaper: "Two cyclists were mauled to death while sleeping near the Russian River yesterday. The bear grabbed one brother and then the other. He gobbled them like a can of sardines. Other campers heard the screams, but nothing could stop the bear from his morning breakfast feast. Services will be held…."

But instead, it wasn't our day to die.

Since my early 20s, through my adventures on six continents—hurricanes, tsunamis, 7.3 earthquakes, 350-pound charging seals in the Galapagos Islands, scuba diving with sharks, mountain climbing, bicycle riding with cars coming up my rear at 70 miles per hour as their drivers send text messages, Australian bush fires, rip-tides, monkeys raining their feces down on me in the Amazon, moose and grizzly bears—so far, they haven't killed me.

But any of them could have killed me.

Should anyone be afraid of dying on an adventure?

Not on your life! Act like a winner. Accept danger. Agree to the unknown and life on its own terms. Go for it. Never worry about living or dying. Keep moving ahead. Think positively to bring all good to you. It's called, "high vibrational frequency living." Charge toward life!

"Let children walk with nature, let them see the beautiful blendings and communions of life and death, their joyous inseparable unity, as taught in woods and meadows, plains and mountains, and streams of our blessed star, and they will learn that death is stingless indeed, and as beautiful as life." John Muir, mountain man, 1881

On a sobering daily note, you may read about someone dying in a traffic accident while coming home from the big game. You hear of a kid succumbing to cancer. A friend fell off a ladder. An average of 900 Americans die annually falling off their bicycles because they didn't wear a helmet. They cracked their skulls. Some people live a short time and others make it a long life. It doesn't make any difference if you're rich, poor, smart, stupid, famous or average. I can name hundreds of famous people who died in their 20's, 30's, 40's, 50's or before their time. You may know some dull people living into their 90's. There is no rhyme or reason to any of it. Life happens.

I personally knew a couple that retired after 40 years at the factory. They bought a motor home to travel to Alaska and around the USA to visit 49 states. The morning before their departure date, the husband walked over to the breakfast table. He grabbed the paper. His wife prepared bacon and eggs on the stove. Suddenly, she heard a thud on the table. She looked around to see her husband slumped over—dead. Life and death happen without cause, warning or understanding.

As the saying goes, "Eat dessert first; life is uncertain."

On a logical note, you can avoid being one of the millions of humans who died but never lived to his or her fullest capabilities. You can avoid staring into a television most of your life. One researcher reported Americans watch television for a total of 15 years of their lives. Millions of Americans suffer a mid-life crisis because they failed to live their dreams or they never discovered their life purpose.

Get your butt out there into the wind, onto the road, up that mountain, down that river, through the deep powder, under the stars and sit by that campfire. Live until you die and if you die while you're living a spectacular life, your spirit will smile all the way through eternity.

CHAPTER 1

Pacific to Atlantic: A Bicycle Journey Across America

The beginning of an epic adventure

"How does it feel to be on the front end of a bicycle journey that promises hardship, true grit, the unknown, and it's bound to test your body, heart, mind and spirit? Long distance bicycle touring challenges you in other ways: patience in dealing with fellow riders who haul their own emotional baggage. Everybody travels with a delicate bag of tricks in their personal backpack. You face constant emotions. You may cry thinking about the loss of a loved one while pedaling. That event may burn deeply into your mind—and the only way to release it—to cry.

"You face hunger like never before in your life. You face laughter like few times in your life as you watch the ongoing human drama play out at every stop, store or campground. You face fellowship

and love/or anger with fellow cyclists. You face decisions that may change your life's trajectory.

"That's the magic of long-distance bicycle adventures. You renew your mind, you tear down and build up your body, you choose your path to the end of the ride. You face crotch rot, sore butt, cramping legs, sweaty body and a voracious appetite. With the magic of bicycling, you become the adventure. Let's see what happens on this ride with this bunch of enthusiastic old men—as they pedaled their way into their own dreams of riding a bicycle from the Pacific Ocean to the Atlantic Ocean." FHW

Robert, Frank, Gerry, Don and Frosty met at Fort Stevens Park, Astoria, Oregon for a ride across America. I met Frank on a ride up the Continental Divide years before. He's a great guy who completed two Ironman Triathlons and other rigorous sporting events. Father, husband and athlete. Gerry, an Irishman with a guitar—sang and played most every day of his life. He provided humor, wisdom and musical energy at sublime moments. He loved a good meal with ample beer. Don, funny, serious, lean, clean and a man of happy countenance. He loved the sense of freedom he found on his bicycle. I never saw a man happier than when he grinned from ear to ear while riding his iron steed. Robert, writer, marathoner and thinker. He writes novels about Icarus and other Greek myths. Philosophical and introspective. He wants to test his legs for a cross continent ride. Frosty, well, I love to ride a bicycle around the globe. What makes me enthusiastic? I am out-of-my-mind-happy each day I get to pedal my bike into a grand adventure. I relish each day that allows me the gift of life and the ability to charge into any kind of adventure.

One note: we're all old men from 65 to 71 with yours truly hitting 72 as you read about this adventure. We sport gray beards, pot bellies, age spots and wrinkles. We've got bad knees, gimpy hips and high blood pressure. We've all been married and divorced, married again or still single, with kids and without kids. One of the group enjoys wealth while the rest enjoy their retirement in financial moderation. Each has a story to tell, and most likely, will tell it along the way. Each of us carries a personality with good and otherwise points. Oh, what the hell! Let's ride!

As we stood with our bikes packed up against the metal hull of a wrecked ship on the Pacific Ocean, waves rolled into the shore with the timing of a clock. Pelicans and seagulls soared on the thermals above us. The blue sky melted into the gray ocean horizon. Sand created endless mosaics on the beach as the eternal winds danced with the universe. For that one moment in time frozen in the pictures we snapped, five guys prepared to strike out across a continent with high expectations to follow their dreams.

As we stood by the wrecked ship, over 100 yards long, it reminded us that we stood near the mouth of the mighty Columbia River in northwestern Oregon. We stood where 700 ships met their tragic fate over the past 200 years. Once the Columbia reaches the ocean, it creates dangerous shoals, sandbars and rip currents. Many a sailor lost his life in those waters. Historians call Astoria the "Ship Graveyard of the Pacific."

The name "Astoria" stems from John Jacob Astor, one of the "Robber Barons" of early America who bought furs from the trappers and sold them to the hat and coat makers in the east. His empire ranged from Canada to the Rockies to the eastern seaboard.

After the pictures, everyone pushed their loaded bikes toward the road to start the journey. Lagging behind, I pulled a small vial out of my panniers to scoop up some Pacific Ocean water. I would repeat that ritual on the Atlantic to put those two vials on my memory shelf back home.

As I pushed my bike through the ankle-deep sand, I remembered that quote by J.K. Rowling, the woman who created Harry Potter. She said, "Let us step out into the night to pursue that flighty temptress—adventure!"

Adventure becomes the temptress. She lures us into her mystical chamber while most of humanity sleeps. She presents us with challenges and opportunities to succeed or fail. That same temptress frustrates the hell out of us at times. She especially lures bicycle riders into her concoctions of heat, sun, rain, cold, sleet, snow and mountain passes. She's got a way of fooling with our minds and spirits. She can make us miserable at any time she chooses. She also dazzles us with astounding sunsets and mountain majesty. All in all, she's a hell of a temptress.

At the same time, she serves each of us tremendous emotional and intellectual freshness. That temptress sends us into uninterrupted marvel within the natural world. On a bicycle adventure, you dig deep on many levels.

On the beach, we met a family that expressed their astonishment at our journey. To those who feel comfortable traveling in a car, the thought of pedaling under their own power totally disarms them. They can't believe it! They don't understand it. Many times, I've heard, "You're crazy! You're totally mad!" Nonetheless, you cannot escape that maddening smile on every cyclist's face as he or she pedals into an amazing adventure on two wheels.

Why do we smile? Simple: each day on a bicycle tour, we enjoy passion, purpose, curiosity, freedom and a new destination. Every life process simplifies down to eating, sleeping, washing and pedaling. What time is it? Who cares! How far will you get? Don't know! Where will you stay? The perfect camp site!

At the beginning of this tour, at our advanced ages, we feel grateful for the ability to undertake such an arduous task. Many our age cannot because of physical limitations.

From Fort Stevens, we pedaled over to Fort Clatsop, the winter home of the Corps of Discovery of the famous Lewis & Clark expedition of 1804-1806. They traveled 4,000 miles by boat, horses and on foot from St. Louis, Missouri to the mouth of the Columbia River and back. President Thomas Jefferson ordered them to meet the Native Americans, map the Louisiana Purchase, catalog every plant and animal, and try to find a river to the Northwest Passage.

My friend, veteran rider, an Irishman, Dave Turner said: Cycling brings you a pure exclusive and overwhelming joy. It's a great feeling of freedom and well-being as your legs propel you over long distances and to new destinations. The soft "hum" of your tires on the road, the pleasure of taking a sip of drink on a really hot day. The small beads of salty sweat that make their way through your bandana and roll down to the tip of your nose and onto your top tube. The moment you reach the summit of a really hard climb and you click into a slightly higher gear at the second you reach the top.

The uplifting feeling you get when a tail wind picks you up and you are propelled effortlessly forward at great speed. Knowing that the burning muscular pain of a long hard climb will be instantly forgotten on the descent and the next day. The expectation of cycling around an uncharted bend not knowing what is around the corner. Hearing heavy rain on the outside of your tent, knowing you're safe and dry. Fixing a puncture and immediately finding somewhere to wash your hands. The smell of a new inner tube.

Knowing that you can cycle over 80 miles day after day after day. Meeting new people, be it other cyclists, other travelers or just folks you just meet along the way. Having a shower and a cold beer after a long cycle. Finding out what is making that annoying "clicking" noise on your bike and eliminating it.

I'm in my seventieth year now and as I write this, I am preparing for a cycle trip across Asia starting in January. I can't wait, that's what cycling does to you. It becomes part of your life, your heart and soul, and once mounted and riding your bicycle, you become at one with yourself, the world and with a little bit of imagination, the universe.

(Don with his fully-loaded touring bike on the first day of the ride.)

CHAPTER 2

The Lewis & Clark Trail

"You know, bicycling isn't just a matter of balance," I said. "It's a matter of faith. You can keep upright only by moving forward. You have to have your eyes on the goal, not the ground. I'm going to call that the Bicyclist's Philosophy of Life." — Susan Vreeland, Clara and Mr. Tiffany

Lewis and Clark with 33 rugged men, one woman and a dog began their journey near St. Louis, Missouri, in May 1804. The Corps of Discovery faced every obstacle and hardship imaginable on their trip. They braved dangerous waters, harsh weather and endured hunger, illness, injury, and fatigue—along with near death by Native Americans and grizzly bears. Along the way, Lewis kept a detailed journal and collected samples of plants and animals he encountered. Lewis and his expedition received assistance during their mission from many of the native peoples they met during their journey westward. The Mandans provided them with supplies during their first winter. At that time that expedition picked up two new members, Sacagawea and Touissant Charbonneau. The two acted as interpreters for the expedition and

Sacagawea, Charbonneau's wife and a Shoshone Indian, helped obtain horses for the group later in the journey.

REACHING THE PACIFIC OCEAN

The Corps of Discovery reached the Pacific Ocean in November of 1805. They built Fort Clatsop and spent the winter in present-day Oregon. On the way back in 1806, Lewis and Clark split up to explore more territory and look for a faster route home. Part of the crew raced down the Yellowstone River. They met up and paddled back to St. Louis for an extraordinary homecoming welcome.

Past that, most of the men received little acclaim and faded into the history books. You may read journals by Lewis, Clark and Sgt. Ordway. Their epic journey defies imagination.

Ironically, the Indians saved them, fed them and rented horses to them. If not for the Native Americans, the Corps would have perished. Consequently, after that time period, the U.S. Army began its extermination of dozens of tribes, their ways of life and their freedom. To this day, Native Americans subsist on Reservations or Internment Camps with poverty, broken cultures and a total loss of their lands and ways of life. Not to mention the Americans introduced booze, which has become Native Americans' drug addiction for hundreds of years. It's painful to watch.

While walking around the grounds of the fort, we strolled past a statue of Indian maiden Sacagawea who saved the men's lives by noticing an Indian chief, who was about to kill all of them, was her brother. She talked him into letting them live. I've visited her gravesite in Fort Washakie, Wyoming on one of my Continental Divide rides.

At the National Park station, a movie shows the hardships of the men during their time at the fort. The men endured bedbugs, fleas, cold, miserable rain daily, rashes, poison ivy, hard cots, stoking the fires 24/7 and trying to forage enough food.

Outside the visitor center, Gerry, with his guitar lashed to the back rack of his bike, engaged with many visitors curious about our ride. Don talked to a number of folks about the trip. Robert and Frank took time to snap pictures and talk to guests at the fort.

The cool thing about our adventure: we anticipated riding our bikes where these guys explored in canoes, on horseback and hiked over mountains. We expected to camp where they camped and see what they saw, for the first time. We anticipated riding 1,500 miles along rivers and across plains that they traversed all the way to Bismarck, North Dakota on the Missouri River. Is that really neat or what?!

Amazingly, we headed our bikes along the same route as those rugged frontiersmen. We stopped in Astoria in the afternoon to enjoy the Columbia River Maritime Museum (www.crmm.org/) that showed the incredible history of the ocean-going ships, fur trade, wrecks, as well as fishing and logging industry of the Northwest. Really, really interesting!

In the late afternoon, filled with history, bursting with information and loaded with food from a couple of groceries—we departed out of Astoria eastward along Route 30 replete with Lewis & Clark signs. Each sign showed two men, one pointing into the distance and one with a flintlock rifle kneeling looking for the right path to follow. Those signs would guide us along the Lewis & Clark Trail for weeks. Additionally, more placards along the Columbia showed us where they camped, where they met Indians and where they nearly died.

We slipped onto the pedals as we got underway for an adventure that would bring challenges to our hearts, minds, spirits and bodies. Whether Marco Polo, Joan of Arc, Captain Cook, Jane Goodall, Ernest Shackleton, Junko Tabei (first woman to climb Mt. Everest), Edmund Hillary, Gertrude Bell, Nellie Bly, Neil Armstrong or Thomas Stevens—adventure calls each of us in a certain way. It calls us to follow that eternal yearning to explore our world. For me, it's a hell of a fountain of creative thought during those long days in the saddle. It's the excitement of meeting exceptionally interesting people, places and animals. As Forrest Gump said, "You never know what's in that box of chocolates." Every day, something new and interesting unfolds on a bicycle tour. I watched my four friends look up the road probably with their own thoughts, own feelings and their own excitement for the days and miles ahead.

For the rest of the afternoon, we rolled along the winding highway, deep in the woods, with glimpses of the vast Columbia River flowing westward. It's pretty much as wild and wilderness-dominated as in Lewis and Clark's time. We enjoyed lush green trees on both sides of the highway with ever-present wildflowers exploding from every berm. Occasionally, deer ran across the road. Dozens of hawks and blackbirds flew everywhere above us.

We camped that night on a small stream with closed campsites. Within 30 minutes, a guy kicked us out. We rolled the bikes through town to meet up with a music festival. A nice lady allowed us campsites on the Columbia River with showers and toilets. One minute we get kicked out of a peaceful campsite on a stream and the next, we're taking showers and talking to festival visitors at a park.

In my journal that night, I wrote: This day, I filled my eyes with beauty from this aboriginal wilderness. I stood on one ocean in order to leave it to reach another ocean. I felt my eyes expand with the onrush of majestic scenery. The sky above me beckoned with its expanse of blue universe garnished with billowy white clouds. My friends laughed. I inhaled great gulps of freedom, mountains, trees, flowers, food and people. Such a journey makes me feel enormously happy.

(Robert, Gerry, Frank and Don standing with their bikes
at Fort Clatsop of the Lewis & Clark Trail.)

CHAPTER 3

Wide Columbia River of the Lewis & Clark Trail

"Bicycling unites physical harmony coupled with emotional bliss to create a sense of spiritual perfection that combines one's body, mind and soul into a moving entity. You, the cyclist, power your steel steed with two spoked metal rims wrapped in rubber tires toward the distant horizon. That faraway place where the sky meets the earth, holds promise on multiple levels. Bicycling allows a person to mesh with the sun, sky and road as if nothing else mattered in the world. At the perfect speed, you flow unerringly toward your destiny. In fact, all your worries, cares and troubles vanish in the rear-view mirror while you bicycle along the highways of the world; you pedal as one with the universe." FHW

To follow up from last night's campground, we rolled toward a 4th of July festival with hundreds of campervans, tents and parties galore—located on the Columbia River. But the lady in charge refused to give us a spot on five acres of mostly open grassland. She proved a stickler for protocol.

She said, "You didn't register online so there is nothing I can do."

Don piped up, "Ma'am, two of us are US Army Veterans. One of our fathers served 27 years in the United States Marine Corps as well as WWII. His father served in WWI. We're the reason for your 4th of July celebration. Surely we deserve five tent spots on these five acres of open space for the night."

"Come to the double gate in five minutes," she said. "I'll talk to the police."

We rolled up to the gate where she spoke to an officer in a police cruiser. He said, "If you follow the exact rules, they can't stay, but they're on bicycles and it's dark and you've got more space than you know what to do with. Besides, I'm an Army veteran. Let'em stay!"

She took us to a grassy spot on the river front and pointed to the bathroom and showers.

"Thank you, ma'am," Don said, with a smile. He tipped his helmet to the police officer. The police officer smiled back at Don and me.

"I find it amazingly odd that someone could be so wrapped up in the rules that she couldn't make such an easy decision," Frank said.

Up the next day, we cooked oatmeal with bananas, hot chocolate and fresh blue berries. It's an amazing feeling waking up to hunger from the night before. Quickly, our bodies burned more calories than we consumed. As we awoke each morning, hunger called. We ate like Kansas wheat combines devouring everything in our paths.

Route 30 rolled through deep woods with shoreline of the Columbia River popping up along the way. We made a side-cut to a Bald Eagle Sanctuary on the river. We watched several bald eagles cruising on their breakfast patrols. We covered 40 miles and turned into a nice town with campsites.

As with all human interaction, and since I organized the trip, I tried to combine five dynamic men, (and I asked women on the ride, too), that would get along well. I thought I did a good job. In the past, I organized trips only to see them go to hell and break up because of incompatible personalities. One thing about a bike tour, you're 'married' to your cycling mates. It can become a love or hate situation.

I'll say one thing about a bike tour: you do not carry your bank account, your job status, your college or educational levels, your age or your accomplishments onto a tour. Your height, weight or looks account for little. You become equal to everyone and they become equal to you. The only thing that makes you viable stems from your ability to pedal a bicycle along a road or up a mountain pass, or into a rainstorm, or into cold regions, or desert heat. No one will give you sympathy if you whine, bitch or complain. Everybody faces their own battles, demons and realities on a long-distance bicycle tour. You cannot toss anger into the air at anyone, because it will come back to you in multiple negative ways. I tried to make that clear at the beginning of the tour. I wrote it out.

That evening, a member of the group got nasty and ugly with yelling at one other in the group for not coming into camp fast enough. He charged that two of us had been screwing off eating watermelon and BS-ing at the store instead of coming to camp. Why it mattered made no sense to me, because I told everyone at the front of the ride that we all go at our own pace and that means: The Pleasure Pace. Don't worry; be happy! Do what you want when you want. Talk to whomever you want.

Take pictures! Camp by yourself or go ahead and hook up later. Everyone enjoyed a cell phone. I made it perfectly clear to make sure everyone enjoyed a fantastic adventure experience.

Then, one of my longtime friends came up to me, "You better kick that son-of-a-bitch off this trip because I'm not riding with him."

"Damn," I said. "I'll talk with him."

As soon as I caught up to the culprit, I said, "Dude, you gotta' apologize to him. Who cares when we got to camp? We weren't eating watermelon. We were waiting for the other dude to get his phone card fixed. Go apologize or you've got bigger problems. He's not someone you can yell at."

"Okay," he said. "I'll apologize."

He apologized, but from that time on, he made one of the crew angry with such an uncalled-for-outburst, and he made me shy away from any conversation. I ride to be out-of-my-mind happy every day! I don't need such anger or tension.

It could have busted up the trip for at least two people. Thankfully, the one dude accepted the apology, and we all got down the road in an okay manner. Lesson to other long-distance touring cyclists: pick your party with care and make rules, written down, that everyone understands.

Avoid making fun of anyone for their weight, food they eat or clothes they wear, or calling them your pet names, or irritating them with negative comments. Differences? Talk in a civil tongue! Never yell at anyone! Because if you toss negative energy into the mix, you will receive multiple consequences. You will lose respect from fellow riders. They will either confront you or fade away from you. Any trip can carry a drama queen or king, and they love to create tension. Avoid becoming a drama king or queen. Also, avoid inviting one on your trip.

We stopped at Shari's Restaurant for dinner. The chocolate pie: delicious! From there, we rolled through Troutdale, Oregon on the Sandy River, to reach, "Gateway to the Columbia River Gorge." That mining and lumber town featured 140 years old buildings on quaint streets with bronze statues in a fountain-filled park.

Century-old architecture gives my eyes a sense of the grandeur of the past. Always brick, always elegant and time makes each building even more beautiful.

We rolled over the Sandy River looking for a campsite.

(The five senior citizen adventure-seekers ready to ride.)

CHAPTER 4

Surprise, Surprise on the Lewis & Clark Trail

"Bicycle adventure creates surprises. They arrive in endless forms. Some delight you and others scare the pants off you. One moment you're riding along and the next, a kangaroo bounds across the road in front of you. At another point, a box turtle makes its way across the road while you ride through the redwoods along the Avenue of the Giants. You stop in amazement at the glory of such a tiny, slow-moving creature amongst giants having lived since the days of the Roman Empire. The wonder of the encounter thrills your spirit, your mind and most of all, your heart. How about the surprise with meeting someone who inspires, encourages and applauds your journey? Remember that evening ride where the sun shone brightly in the west while your shadow danced 50 feet across the highway and played on the meadow? The surprises continue as long as you keep pedaling. And, how about that huge canine racing out of the

driveway to chew off a piece of your leg? We can all do without that surprise!

"No matter what, your pedaling adventures create the most unique moments at the most mundane of times. Did you write them down in your journal? How about that double rainbow rising over the canyon as you pedaled through the Rocky Mountains? What about that sprinkler that caught you in the dead of night because you stealth-camped in a church backyard or in a rest area or anywhere that you didn't expect such a surprise? You learned from that one! If you see green grass, you know sprinklers must be under the green blades. How about the time you saw a car run over a deer crossing the road? Just brought tears to your eyes! You felt so hopeless. Unfortunately, you can't un-see such events. I remember my first ride through Asia. I saw starving people and dead people crumpled in the streets. Just blew my mind, hurt my soul and crushed my spirit.

"At some point, you rack up 1,000 surprises over a lifetime. As long as you pedal, life thrusts special moments of joy, sorrow, amazement, pain and hope into your heart and into your eyes.

"Whatever lessons life offers, grab them, hold them, learn from them and move forward toward the distant horizon. Each moment teaches. Each event makes you wiser. Each carries a price, some anguish, some reward and/or unusual benefit. As you sit by the campfire at night, the stars twinkle. The flames flicker and the smoke curls into the night air. You sit under the grand cathedral of the universe. Your friends devour their dinners or drink a few *beers. Jokes and stories abound. You glare into the campfire with the magic of the universe looking back at you." FHW*

After passing through the Old West town of Troutdale, Oregon, we crossed over a 100-year-old silver steel bridge still carrying cars and trucks in this modern age. While we felt excited about riding into the Columbia River Gorge the next day, we watched the long shadows of the trees crossing the road. We pedaled along the river as the sun began setting in the west.

"Where's a campsite?" Frank asked.

"Gees," said Don. "We're burning daylight pretty fast. We better find a camp-spot within 20 minutes or we're camping on gravel on the side of this road."

"Let's get movin' mates," said Gerry. "I'm ready for sleep."

"Too bad we won't get to celebrate the 4th of July with fireworks and campfire," I said. "Bad timing!"

A mile down the road, a day-use-only park featured plenty of picnic tables, but rangers would kick us out in the night. As we stood by the entrance, a pickup truck with a couple stopped at the stop sign to turn right in the same direction we were headed.

"Sir," I said. "Any chance you know of any place five guys could camp along this road? We're heading cross country and tomorrow, we're heading into the Columbia River Gorge."

"Sorry," he said. "But there aren't any camping places along here. Just cottages with summer owners. You won't find much until you climb into the higher country along the river. Sorry about that."

"Thanks so much," I said. "We'll bed down on the side of the highway if we can't find a place."

They drove off. Robert, Don and Gerry rode into the day-use park trying to find a hidden spot in the trees to camp.

Frank and I cranked along the road with the Sandy River on our right. We lamented no place to camp among cottages with people and private property. We kept pedaling under a dense canopy of trees for another mile until the road began to climb. Up ahead, that same pickup with the man and wife sat beside the highway. We kept cranking until we reached them about a half-mile away. The man rolled down the window.

"Hey, we've been thinking," he said. "We've got a big farm house about two miles from here with a big flower garden front yard for tents. You guys are welcome to stay the night. We've got showers, lots of food, campfire and fireworks going off. We felt you might like to celebrate the 4th of July with us rather than camping out on gravel."

"This is Frank and my names if Frosty," I said, extending my hand for a handshake. "We'd be delighted. I'll phone the guys."

"Here's a map to get to our house," he said. "I'm Brian and this is my wife, April."

"Oh," Frank said, gasping with delight. "We're honored by your offer."

"Hope you got big appetites because we've got plenty of food," Brian said. "I noticed that your one friend was carrying a guitar case on his bike. Am I right?"

"You sure are," said Frank. "He plays every song from the 50's on up. He plays for a band in Ireland. He's a superb singer."

"We have quite a few guitar players at our party," said Brian. "Should make for a good time. We'll wait for your arrival."

"Thanks a million," I said.

Frank called Don on the cell phone.

"Dude, we got showers and tent sites, food, fireplace and fireworks," said Frank. "Get your butts up here so we can start the party."

"Roger that, huh?" said Don, with a note of confusion or surprise in his voice.

Shortly, they pedaled up the hill toward us. We told them the story. Everyone agreed we just lucked into a really good deal.

Just as darkness overtook us, we pedaled into a wide yard surrounded by a dazzling display of flowers the likes you wouldn't see except for a botanical garden. Every color in a Sherwin-Williams paint shop jumped out at us from bushes, flower gardens and pots. A golf course green lawn provided camping-spots in the yard filled with flowers. We smelled the sweet scents of petunias, tiger lilies, roses galore, mountain flowers, iris and two dozen more flowers.

Brian and April walked out, "Welcome to my parent's home, Ed and Coreen. My mom loves flowers and created this paradise. Showers are inside that corner door. When you're showered up, come to the back yard for barbecue, mashed potatoes, salad, fruits, pies and all the fixings. My friends already have their guitars out around the campfire. Make yourselves at home."

All five of us looked around at each other with wonderment. How in the daylights did five scroungy, stinky, sweaty, scruffy, dilapidated old fogeys ride their bicycles into a dream like this?

"Let's git 'er done boys," said Robert. "Foods awaitin'!"

After showers, we walked to the back patio to see a spread of food set for Viking warriors. A beautiful fire pit roared with flames ripping into the night air. Two guys played guitars while a number of women sang along with them. Trees surrounded the yard and a big meadow featured a number of lights from a fireworks crew.

"Holy catfish," said Don. "This is a spread set for a king and his army. Where do I start?"

"Grab some plates and silverware," said Brian.

After 30 minutes of gorging ourselves on more food than we ever imagined, folks settled down around the campfire for a songfest. Everyone enjoyed their favorite beverage. Gerry cracked out his guitar to join the fest. Turns out, he proved the best guitarist and singer of the group. He sang Willie Nelson's "On the Road Again" and "Riding on the City of New Orleans", and "Time in a Bottle" and dozens more. He just mesmerized everyone around the campfire.

Later, fireworks lit up the sky. Everybody cheered as Roman candles exploded everywhere across the ink-black of space.

We lived one of those nights that you never want to end. Friendship, good food, good drinks, conversation, guitars, singing, blazing fire and the energy of the universe coursing through everyone's bodies. Around 1:00 a.m., I called it a night. I walked back to my tent, jumped into my sleeping bag, and fell fast asleep.

Next morning, we stepped up to an amazing breakfast buffet with fried eggs, oatmeal, fruit bowl, milk, cereal, toast, butter and jam, pancakes and sausages.

"How in the daylights did we walk into this one?" asked Don.

That's the question every cyclist probably asks when such a "surprising" moment jumps up and grabs him or her. Who planned this? Why me? What do you do to thank the Jensen's? In the end, you pass it forward.

During breakfast, everybody took pictures. After handshakes and hugs, we waved goodbye as we pedaled out of the driveway and onto the road. Within moments, that incredible surprise faded into our rearview mirrors.

The one thing I've found about bicycle travel; you can't tarry with yesterday and you can't stop tomorrow from coming at you full speed at 12 miles per hour. All you can do: enjoy the creative energy of the universe and pedal down adventure highway.

(Gerry playing his magical guitar around the
campfire on the 4th of July celebration.)

CHAPTER 5

Columbia River Gorge with Fabled Multnomah Falls

"Have you ever enjoyed such a good time at some event that you wanted it to last forever? Last night, with the campfire, fireworks and music players—a sheer songfest with Gerry Mulroy with his magical guitar—a certain magic swallowed us into emotional bliss. We didn't want it to end.

"About the only things that don't end: ocean waves, soft breezes, sunsets and changing seasons. While you may pedal through them, you can't stop them. While you enjoy that one 'moment' of sheer joy, another 'moment' awaits around the next bend in the road. You may never define the next moment. It surprises you! It arrives from every countenance of life, people, animals and weather.

"Nonetheless, you can't tarry with yesterday. Thankfully, today, you enjoy a camera or video for pictures that recover that moment. You display it on the screen and share it with friends.

"But in the end, you must move forward into the future. While you may not 'create' a moment, the very fact that you pedal down the road, that action thrusts you into another unique event in your life. Relish it, live it and smile that life treats you well. You represent living poetry in motion." FHW

Next morning, we turned right into an immediate steep climb as we pedaled into the Columbia River Gorge. Our flags fluttered as we hammered into higher country. Gerry and Frank talked about the surprise party last night. Laughing, joking and sharing! You couldn't have written it better out of a movie script. While movies come from someone's imagination, our surprise party last night arrived on a random-chance party platter.

At the end of the summer, as a "Thank you", I sent the Jensen family a copy of my book, **Living Your Spectacular Life**, as well as 20 of my "Spirit of Adventure" greeting cards. I thanked them profusely for their kindness. I know the rest of the guys did the same thing. It's important to thank people for their generosity, and even more important, to pay it forward. Sandi and I host touring cyclists at our home on Route 40, in Golden, CO, which rolls beside us as a major bicycle touring thoroughfare from San Francisco to the East Coast. www.WarmShowers.org We've hosted Chinese, Dutch, Irish, Aussies, Germans, Swedes, Brits and more. It's nice because those world travelers discover that ordinary Americans present the decency, kindness and goodness of America.

We rolled through thick trees on Historic Route 30 of the Columbia River Gorge. The serpentine highway threaded into higher country along the Columbia River. Wildflowers graced our way on both sides of the highway. Crows and hawks, along with sparrows flew in all directions. White clouds skidded across a deep blue sky. At the top, the road leveled along a ridge to pass by a rest-stop with a view of the Columbia River into the distance. The early morning sun sparkled with millions of diamonds of its surface. We pulled into the rest area titled, "Women's Forum Overlook."

"Would you look at that," said Frank. "It's astounding! You can see for 30 miles up the river with thick forests on both sides. It's the same as it was when Lewis & Clark paddled their canoes down this river."

"But they didn't have a clue as to where they were or what would happen to them next," said Don. "This is rugged wilderness. Good grief; this is amazing."

Before us, the river valley stretched endlessly into the distance. It swallowed our imaginations with its vast dark green wilderness, "too silent to be real." (Gordon Lightfoot) How did Lewis & Clark manage to keep their wits about them? They might as well have been exploring the same territory as you saw in the movie "Avatar." The Columbia River stretched a half-mile wide in places. Grizzlies awaited, brown bear, Native Americans and a whole lot of mosquitos!

We rolled out of there after a dozen pictures and talking to other tourists. Of course, every tourist comes over to talk with us about our journey. Most show astonishment at our endeavors.

"How far do you guys travel daily?" one asked.

"About 50 miles in the mountains and 70 miles on the flats," Frank said.

"What happens when it rains?" another asked.

"We pretend we're ducks," said Don, chuckling.

"Can't be too much fun in the rain," the tourist said.

"Out of three months on the road," said Don. "We might ride in two days of rain, so it's not such a bad deal. If we don't like it, we can camp out in a motel and read books."

"Where's your support vehicle?" one lady asked.

"Fully self-contained," said Gerry. "Just like Lewis & Clark."

"Don't you get sweaty and dirty?" she asked.

"We carry shower bags to take four-minute showers before bedtime," I said. "Love to hit the sack fresh and clean."

Not far from the first stop, we reached the "Crown Point Vista House," a circular tower built for tourists back in the 1930's. It featured pictures and history of the amazing "Columbia River Gorge Road" that we rode upon in the 21st century. The most amazing thing about the road: you can't tell it's there in the woods. It's always under the tree line, so it's essentially invisible.

We dropped quickly down 1,000 feet to a section of the road that carried us to seven major waterfalls that erupted out of the wilderness. We passed La Tourell and Bridal Veil Falls all the way up to Multnomah Falls. From the tour guide, Multnomah Falls boasted the second highest continuous waterfalls in the United States behind Niagara Fall: 622 feet!

As we neared the falls, the traffic jammed backward for several miles. What did we do? We rolled past all of it to save ourselves an hour or more waiting at the end of the line.

One motorist rolled down his window, "Man, I wish I was riding with you guys. This traffic sucks."

The falls didn't disappoint. A short walk past hundreds of tourists gave us a bird's eye view of the falls cascading from the edge of the valley rim to a pool. Across the narrows, a stone bridge cut the entire picture of the falls in half.

"Wow," said Frank. "That's incredible! It's so pristine. It's so lush with that bottom pool so blue. Man, this makes this day an "A+" in my book."

"No question," Gerry said. "I need to write a song about these waterfalls."

Later in the day, we rolled eastward along the Columbia River until we reached the Cascade Locks. Engineers built the locks to give ships passage to the higher waters of the Columbia. Today, all that remains: huge concrete foundations.

We pulled into a campground to discover a small Adventure Cycling group crossing America—led by Tom Middaugh and Kolianna. They invited us to dinner and their campfire. As luck would have it, Tom played guitar. Gerry played guitar. They pulled out their magical musical instruments. All of a sudden, another music festival erupted along the Columbia River. I think in the Lewis & Clark Expedition, one of the guys carried a harmonica. He made music. That night Tom and Gerry made fabulous music with songs from the Beatles, Willie Nelson, Waylon Jennings, Simon and Garfunkel, The Supremes and so much more.

We sang our hearts out.

Later, we walked down to a beer pavilion near the water to drink a brew and eat more pizza. Amazingly while cycling, you can eat a first dinner, and if someone offers more food, you can eat a second dinner, too. Devouring food becomes a way of life on a bicycle tour.

(This is the second tallest continuously falling waterfall in America. Multnomah
Falls is located along the Columbia River Gorge. It drops 622 feet into a pool.
A bridge connects two sides of the canyon to give a fantastic view for tourists.)

CHAPTER 6

Columbia River Gorge, a Ride Through History

"*You never know who you might meet on a bicycle tour. That person may change your life. They might make a comment that enlightens you or disturbs you. At the same time, you might inspire someone without knowing it. Or, some person may jump into your world for a moment and jump out just as fast.*

"*Yesterday, while enjoying the splendor of Multnomah Falls, I parked my bike along the stone fence leading up the walk to the falls. As my friends and I returned from taking pictures, I stood next to my bike "Condor" chatting and devouring an ice cream cone. As usual, Gerry told a few of his Irish jokes while Don and I stood by him, laughing. A man walked up.*

"*Are you the owner of this bike?" he asked. "Is that your sign on that bike about riding from the Pacific to the Atlantic?*"

"Yes sir," I said.

"Are you really bicycling from the Pacific Ocean to the Atlantic?" he asked.

"Yes sir," I said.

"That does it," he said. "I've been thinking about riding my bike across America for more than 20 years. You've just given me the courage to do it, too. I'm going to ride across America next summer. I'm not going to waste another summer of my retirement. Thanks for giving me the courage."

"Gosh, you're welcome," I said as he shook my hand and walked away. FHW

Quickly in the morning, the Adventure Cycling crew packed up and headed out. Last to go, the cook, Kolianna dressed up in her bicycle garb and swung her leg over the top tube.

"Thanks for the veggie dinner," I said.

"Thank Gerry for his guitar playing and great songs around the campfire last night," she said. "That was a fun songfest."

"You're the best," I said. "Happy travels."

"Same to you guys," she said, as she pedaled up the hill toward the highway.

In an instant, she left our lives. In a split second, she moved onward into her own life. She's one of those wanderers who loves adventure more than comfort, more than security and more than the constancy of day-to-day living at home.

We ate breakfast, packed and headed eastward into that vast wilderness of the Columbia Gorge. Sheer, unadulterated beauty surrounded us all day long. We rolled high on the valley ridge only to descend back down along the river. Always the sparkling waters of the river! Always the eternal green of the trees! Along the way, we saw flowers lilting in the breezes and reflecting their colors with the blazing sunshine. Yellow, blue, orange, white, red, topaz, purple, pink, and more! Emerson said, "God laughs in flowers!" God seemed to laugh along every mile of our journey. Above, hawks soared in the sky, and in the meadows, deer grazed on summer grasses.

At one point, we pedaled through a cherry orchard. Tons of cherries grew on the public highway domain. We grabbed fresh, juicy cherries right off the trees.

"What a bonanza," said Don.

"Maybe we could set up camp here," Gerry said. "And eat ourselves into cherry heaven."

"Too early in the day, dude," Frank said.

Near the end of the Gorge, the paved path turned into a steep cement stairway. We unpacked our bikes and carried them down the steps. We helped each other to make sure we didn't drop the bikes. After some arduous step-up climbing and down-climbing, we set the bikes back up on the trail.

Near the end of the day, we rolled along some sheer cliffs high above the river. The terrain showed massive brown cliffs with deep drops into small canyons. We rolled through picture taking paradise.

At the end of the ridge, an overlook parking lot showed a fabulous horseshoe road below that wound downward toward the next small town named "Dalles" which meant 'small ripples' on the river. We continued along Historic Route 30 of the Columbia River Gorge. I directed everyone to position themselves on the highway to ride into that horseshoe bend for the video and camera shots.

"It's daylight, we ride," said Don.

They flew around the back edge of the viewpoint to make their way into the horseshoe curve. I snapped some fabulous pictures of their descent.

After taking great videos and pictures, I jumped on my bike for the ride down into the horseshoe. I must hand it to the engineers of the Columbia River Gorge: they created an extremely beautiful and non-invasive road through stark wilderness that stuns visitors with its beauty to this day.

Just imagining those brave 33 men on their Corps of Discovery journey astounds me with their courage, their tenacity and their bravery. It seems every era features a Captain Cook who sailed around the world his entire life. Or, Sir Edmund Hillary and Norgay Tensing who conquered Mount Everest. Or, Amelia Earhart who flew the Atlantic solo and attempted to fly around the world. Or the thousands of unknown men and women climbing, bicycling, sailing, scuba diving, rafting and proceeding through their lives with the same intent of discovering the world on their own.

It's pretty heady stuff to explore the world during your lifetime. Right now, if you're reading this history of our journey, I hope you gain something from the spirit of adventure. I hope you become that man or woman who steps up to talk with us, and then, decides to embark on your own adventure around your state, country or the world. You might like to backpack the Colorado Trail, or Pacific Coast Trial, or the Appalachia Trail. You may decide to climb all the 14ers in the USA. You might scuba dive the Great Lakes or the Gulf of Mexico. Or, perhaps kayak the great rivers. How about canoeing the Mississippi River?

Those adventures await you. Answer the call in your own way.

We rolled into Dalles for camp. Dinner never tasted so good after so much climbing and descending.

"Good day today, boys," said Don.

"A very good day," said Frank.

That night, we enjoyed a campfire much like those men who traversed North America back in 1804-06. It's a heady feeling to camp where they camped, to gaze at the same trees and watch the flow of the same rivers.

Have you ever sat by the campfire?
When the wood has fallen low?
And the embers start to whiten,
Around the campfire's crimson glow?

With a full moon high above you,
That makes silence doubly sweet,

And the night sounds all around you,
That makes the spell complete.

Tell me were you ever nearer,
To the land of heart's desire,
Than when you sat there thinking,
With your face toward the fire?

(Our gang riding the big S-curve through the Columbia
River Gorge. Located at the eastern end of the Gorge, this
horseshoe curve offers a dramatic ride for cyclists.)

CHAPTER 7

The Joy of Tailwinds

"Where are you guys camping tonight?" strangers asked. "The perfect spot," I replied. "Something always turns up. No matter what, a touring cyclist rarely worries about where he or she might stay the night. It's a matter of trusting the camping gods as to our destiny each day on the road. Perfect spots might mean the parking lot in back of a church or school. I've camped in farmer's fields, construction sites, junk yards, in the middle of San Francisco, grave yards, front yards of suburbanites, public parks, along rivers and streams, baseball fields, abandon buildings, drainage ditches and a hundred other surprising locations. Each one provides a new adventure. With a shower bag, dinner over a one-burner stove, tent, sleeping bag and air mattress—I sleep with the stars as my cathedral and the full moon as my nightlight." FHW

Last night, we rolled over the bridge into Washington State. We attempted to camp by the Columbia River, but signs prohibited it. We asked a vagabond where we might camp.

"Just go to the next dirt road on your right and follow it down the hill to a parking lot," he said. "You can slide by the gate and follow the trail to an abandoned park. It's got picnic tables, a clear pond and plenty of trees. No one ever goes there anymore. It's called Hess Park."

"Roger that," Frank said.

Sure enough, we pedaled into a quaint, wooded paradise with tables and a pond for bathing. Everybody took a bath. We sat at the tables cooking dinner and filling up our journals with the events of the day. It even featured outhouses. Of course, we used bio-degradable soap and left the place spotless.

Around the campfire, Gerry wanted to hear one of my "epic" moments while on tour. He pulled out his guitar to provide some dramatic music for this story, "Leap for Life."

Heading east on Route 92 out of Provo, Utah, Sandi and I cranked hard through the afternoon. Above us, craggy 10,000-foot peaks poked into a cloudy sky. It was so hot, we dripped our way through deep canyons. We stopped for a rest area at a turnout.

"Sure is a lot different than the salt flats," Sandi said, sucking on her water bottle.

"My legs are feeling this hill," I added, with a sweat bead ready to drop off my nose. "Guess they forgot about climbing after so long on the flats."

"It's prettier up here."

"Sure is," I said. "These mountains inspire me."

A few minutes later, we coasted down a steep incline, only to climb again. I dislike losing altitude, only to climb again, but it's useless to fight it. We coasted through endless curves. Ahead of us, on the crest of a climb, a small boulder had fallen onto the road. I decided to move it off the pavement, so it wouldn't smash a car's undercarriage to bits.

"Give me a minute Sandi," I said, laying my bike on the side of the road. "I'm gonna' get this rock off the road. Could get somebody killed."

"I need a rest anyway," she said.

At that moment, another small rock cracked down from overhead. It bounced across the road before slamming into the guardrail.

"Looks like we're under some falling rock," I said, hoisting the boulder to the side of the road.

"LOOK OUT!" Sandi yelled.

A shower of small rocks bounced across the road. I looked up to see where it originated.

"Look at that," I said, pointing upward.

"It's a Bighorn sheep," Sandi said. "He's knocking those rocks down on us. He looks like he's in a tight spot."

About 100 feet above us, a Bighorn stood on a ledge, haltingly, because the path ended. His massive curled horns swept back from the top of his head. He looked a bit pensive as he nearly leaped forward, but stopped.

"He's gonna' jump, but there's no place to go," Sandi said.

"Unless it's that ledge above him."

"That's gotta' be more than 15 feet away and higher!"

"Maybe that's why he's hesitating."

Without a second pause, the ram coiled his body before launching himself up and out to the ledge above him. His trajectory rose upward, but not quite high enough to reach the higher rock. Instead, his two front feet slid like skids on a flat rock, and one rear leg caught the edge of the ledge. He was about to fall 100 feet to his death before our eyes. But in a split second, with his one rear leg locked onto the ledge, he threw his front legs upward and thrust his head back. He kicked with his one back leg to launch himself upside down, his hooves pointed to the sky, back toward his original ledge. While in the middle of his flight back, he twisted his body like a cat before landing.

But again, only his front legs made the lower ledge, and his one rear hoof reached the rock. His front legs skidded onto the ledge again, but his rear end was not going to make it. With only a split second left before he slipped off the ledge, he bellowed as he kicked hard with his one back leg that had made the ledge. That thrust kicked the back of his body upward and with the momentum of the leap, spun his rump around until he fell sideways onto the ledge. He rested there stunned. Several minutes later, he stood up, grunted, and walked back the other way.

"My God," Sandi gasped.

"I felt that," I said.

John Muir, America's first environmentalist and creator of our national park systems said it best: "How many hearts with warm red blood in them are beating under the cover of the woods, and how many teeth and eyes are shining? A multitude of animal people, intimately related to us, but whose lives we know almost nothing, are as busy about their own lives as we about ours."

While bicycling, I roll quietly into the last of the silence. It allows me to peek into their lives—often.

"Hell of a tale, Frosty," said Don. "I can't wait for a moment like that to happen to me."

"Count on it," I said, confidently. "You're going to ride into several epic moments on this ride."

Next morning, as Hess Park faded in our rear-view mirrors, we stopped at a fruit processing plant for water. As we rode toward Route 14, we faced a 40 to 50 mph head and side winds. When the trucks passed, the draft blew us into the gravel. One blew Frank off his bike for a hard crash. I nearly crashed twice with the force of the side wind. It felt very unnerving to pedal into such a wild tempest. Once we reached Route 14 east-bound, a rip-roaring tail wind blew us down the road.

"Dude," said Don. "We should be getting tailwinds pretty quick."

"I hope so," said Frank. "I can't take any more crashes."

"I feel tailwinds about to change our day," said Robert.

As miserable as headwinds make a cyclist, tailwinds, well, let me tell you about tailwinds. They thrill every cell in my body. They push me down the road like an eagle. I feel like I'm soaring above the land with a sense of freedom, quite unexplainable. Yet, so good, so kind, so fabulous! My muscles yearn to press on those cranks. I spread my arms out to feel like a bird in flight. I smile from ear to ear. My blood cells celebrate in every section of my body. I think they dance to the music of the wind. The taste of life and all its wonder spills into my soul. Tailwinds excite my mind. They make me feel like a million dollars. Give me tailwinds. That makes me the happiest man on this planet.

How do you describe tailwinds for anyone who hasn't flown with them on a bicycle? It's kinda' like when you walk through an airport. On long stretches, they offer a horizontal elevator to whisk you to your flight gate at two to three times your regular walking speed. As you step onto the horizontal elevator, you immediately enjoy an "assist" that rushes you along the corridor. It feels energizing as if some unknown entity takes you in its arms. It feels good to either relax or keep walking to travel ever faster to your boarding gate. That's what tailwinds do for a cyclist: an invisible assistance, in this case, Mother Nature, revs up the pleasure of the journey.

After we climbed 500 feet, we looked out over the vast Columbia River. It featured white caps being blown hard eastward. Blue sky dominated. Hard winds ripped the grasses nearly flat, pointing eastward. We followed the serpentine road into the rising sun. It's amazing how your mind changes when the ride changes from gut busting leg work to easy going tailwinds.

As we looked out over the vast expanse of the Columbia River, the vastness swallowed our confidence. Our eyes encountered rugged terrain on both sides of the river with blue sky doming over the entire procession of nature. The Lewis & Clark discovery team played an ever-greater understanding on our minds. The sheer enormity of their quest stunned us. We gazed across the immense stretch of wilderness for as far as our eyes could see.

Knowing that a member of the Corps of Discovery could be killed by a grizzly bear at any stop must have been sobering. In 1804, 50,000 grizzlies roamed North America. Today, only 2,000 grizzlies survive.

Daily, hunger plagued the explorers in the winters. Native Americans could kill them in a heartbeat. And mosquitos! Good grief, they sucked blood until a man might go crazy. To be in close proximity with 33 other men 24/7, even ones you don't like, must have been a test of patience. Yet they pushed 4,000 miles into the unknown wilderness. All the way down the Columbia River to the Pacific.

The fact that we pedaled in their footsteps at a speed pretty much like the speed of their journey—gave us a greater understanding.

Most travelers today travel more miles in one hour than touring cyclists travel in a full day. The slowness of our travel allows a totally different orientation for time and distance. Such a pace allows for meditation of the pedals. Humanity may function better at the speed of a bicycle.

Over 200 years after the Lewis and Clark expedition, we pedaled our bicycles 50 miles a day with food and water assured. We never feared death by a grizzly or arrows. We might suffer being run over by a car, but probably not.

We pushed toward Roosevelt, a small town on the river, in 103-degree heat. Above us on both sides of the river valley, hundreds of white, tall, wind turbines turned the tempest into electricity.

We pulled into the only restaurant in Roosevelt. The cook made pancakes, strawberry shakes, burgers, salads and French fries. We gobbled them down, ate them up and drank a few beers.

Later, we rolled a mile down to the city park to enjoy a freshly mowed lawn, showers and the Columbia River at our tent flaps. Gerry played a few songs on his guitar while we cooked dinner and sang along with him. Electrical plug-ins charged all our electronics.

The host, a plumber from Chicago, living in a motorhome, told us how he sailed around the world for 13 years before catching Dengue Fever that degraded his joints. He now takes life one day at a time.

One camper walked up, "What are a bunch of gray-haired old men like you guys doing riding bicycles across the country?"

Don said, "We keep pedaling to stay one step ahead of old age and two steps away from death."

"Fair enough," he said. "I hope I'm in as good a shape as you guys when I reach 70."

We rolled hard the next day from Roosevelt to Umatilla, Oregon. The air proved hotter than two mice having sex in a wool sock on a July day in Phoenix, Arizona! Sweat, sweat and more sweat. Drink, drink, drink and more guzzling of the water bottles. As fast as we could drink fluids, the winds and heat sucked moisture out of us.

Finally, in Umatilla, we crossed back over another bridge to a campground near the water.

As a surprise, a woman named Judi walked over to our table with a tray of strawberries, wine, cheese and crackers.

"You boys hungry?" she asked.

"Like a Kansas combine in the early morning," said Don.

We munched on her treats. Gerry pulled out his guitar for a few songs to keep her attention. Great lady with an interesting history of being a walnut plantation owner. She thought we were crazy for riding across America. We liked her anyway.

On this journey, Gerry Mulroy made every stop a mystical, magical, musical moment. His golden voice poured the words into the evening air. His hands strummed that guitar like a virtuoso at the symphony. Every woman who heard his songs fell in love with him. The rest of us hung on for sheer delight. Gerry sang a Willie Nelson classic:

"Riding on the City of New Orleans…Illinois Central, Monday morning rail…Fifteen cars and fifteen restless riders…three conductors, 25 sacks of mail…all along that southbound odyssey, the train pulled out at Kankakee…and rolls along past houses, farms and fields.

"Passin' trains that have no names, and graveyards full of old black men, and the graveyards of rusted automobiles. Good morning, America, how are you? Say don't you know me? I'm your native son.

"I'm the train they call the City of New Orleans, and I'll be gone five hundred miles when the day is done…."

We sang that song and many others with Gerry leading the lyrics and strumming his magical guitar. It shows that music and the music makers create joy in our lives.

As I closed the zipper on my tent that night, I felt good about life. I felt joy at the tailwinds that day. I felt camaraderie with my cycling mates. Even with my old muscles letting me know that they didn't appreciate so much work, they relaxed. Same with my bones! They didn't care for the constant pounding of the pedals, but they carried me through another day. In the end, we all ride in a disposable space suit made of skin, bones and blood. If we take care of it; it will take care of us.

(Gerry and Don taking a break along the Columbia River. Their
beards turned grayer and longer as the journey proceeded.)

CHAPTER 8

Interesting Discussions from Umatilla to Waitsburg, Washington

"Gut level conversations! You get into them during a bicycle tour with your fellow riders, and/or, strangers who approach you. Some need to express their feelings while others articulate their anger. A bike tour digs down into your soul. It exposes your mind and heart to the harsh realities of life as well as the ephemeral beauties of living on the road. I don't know about you, but I remember my youth, my school years, my marriage and divorce, my failures and successes, and my utter confusion and exasperation as to why life on this planet appears to be full of contradictions.

"One minute I pedal up to the Wall of China, and the next, I pedal to the Taj Mahal. At other times, I ride through the Outback sweating like a pig, and at others, I ride across the Golden Gate

Bridge. To ride up to the Roman Coliseum or pedal to the Parthenon in Greece—all give a sense of wonder. At the same time, behind the Taj Mahal, millions of pieces of plastic float in the river. Millions in poverty and misery throughout India. Endless wars being waged around the planet! Hardship, disease and hopelessness abound on every continent. It stuns my mind and exasperates my senses. If humans didn't support armies with enormous costs, all of humanity could live fabulous lives with education, housing, clean water and ample food.

"I wonder how and/or why I received the lucky lotto ticket for enjoying a healthy, happy and productive life. When, at the same time, I've seen millions living in the dregs of misery. That's some of the thoughts that cruise through my mind during my pedaling down the road of life." FHW

As fate surprises you, all sorts of conversations pop up. We met Ken, a retired Los Angeles teacher, who said the schools suffered from students speaking 100 different languages. American kids can't speak Spanish and can't handle the tension directed toward themselves. Ken spoke about 90,000 homeless people living under blue tarps and ragged tents.

"It's really sad," he said. "Nobody's figured out a way to solve the problem. There's 11,000 homeless in San Francisco. Tens of thousands of people suffer from drug abuse, alcoholism and mental health issues."

A retired police officer told us that it's not safe in Los Angeles and San Francisco as those cities slide toward pockets of third world slums.

You kinda' slip away from such conversations with a sense of your own good fortune. I lived for a time in a 30-foot trailer as a youth with four siblings. Yes, we experienced poverty, but we ate enough food, attended school and moved forward in life. If you're a baby boomer, I'll bet you might tell your own story of the good, not so good and hard times in your life. We each carry a story. Thankfully, we each can change that story toward the positive side of living.

We rolled eastward on Route 730 to connect to Route 12 heading into Walla Walla, Washington.

The smooth roadway offered rugged brown mountain cliff faces above us. Railroad tracks on the other side provided long freight trains winding their way up and down the Columbia River. It's all about commerce and the trading of goods. On the high ridges, hundreds of white wind turbines slashed at the sky while producing electricity.

Along the route, I snapped photographs from high cliffs of the guys riding along the river. At intervals of flat land, we saw wheat, bean and hay fields growing in patchwork green spaces. At one point in the 1930's, enormous combines, pulled by 33 horse teams, cut the wheat in huge swaths.

Turning onto Route 12, we reached Walla Walla by mid-afternoon. We stopped for lunch at a railroad station turned into a bistro. After lunch, we visited a bicycle shop.

During the ride, I suggested that everyone regularly check their nuts and bolts on their racks. Check their cables. Check their tires. Check pressures. Check their chains. Oil their chains. Check to secure all gear at all times. Check for dangling bungees. I've seen good bikes go down for the count for lack of maintenance. I've witnessed bungees snap spokes when the hooks got caught in the wheel.

Before the ride, I suggested new Schwalbe Marathon Tour Plus tires for everyone. I know excellent touring tires and those Schwalbe's give the best ride, toughest wear and are puncture proof in most cases. At the tire shop, I noticed Robert's tires needed replacement. And, since we faced huge stretches of country in Montana, I suggested two new tires and carrying a spare.

He declined my suggestions. At that point, with 47 years of world touring experiences, I figured I better bow out of the suggestion business.

We decided to push on toward Waitsburg, Washington, another 25 miles. We rolled through stunning scenery. We enjoyed a quilted tapestry of lavender flower fields, hay, wheat, green beans, onions, carrots and other crops. As we approached 75 miles in distance that day, and exhausted from the heat and hills, we coasted five miles into

Waitsburg for a fantastic camp at the fairgrounds with toilets and showers via hoses.

In Waitsburg for dinner and beers, we discovered a mostly abandoned city right out of the 1800's. The town offered superb architecture of office buildings and interesting bronze statues. Old advertising paintings marked the sides of brick buildings. The town featured hardware, grocery, bars and legal offices. At the T-intersection, a bronze statue of a teacher looked down at a student reading at a round table. Down the street, we encountered a statue of three dock workers hauling beans bags on a wheelbarrow. It felt like stepping back in time.

(Don and Frank play with the guys in this sculpture
on the streets of Waitsburg, Washington.)

CHAPTER 9

Old America with Tractors, Combines and Plows

"The cyclist creates everything from almost nothing, becoming the most energy-efficient of all animals and machines and, as such, has a genuine ability to challenge the entire value system of a society. The bicycle may be too cheap, too available, too healthy, too independent and too equitable for its own good. In an age of excess, it is minimal and has the subversive potential to make people happy in an economy fueled by consumer discontent." Jim McGurn

Sometimes, you hate to leave a special place where something grabbed your heart, touched your emotions, and perhaps caught your soul. Waitsburg, Washington became that place for this touring cyclist. Simplicity permeated every section of town. The solid oak hardware floors creaked under my shoes when I walked across them. The cobbled streets spoke to me about a simpler time. The long, tall windows in the buildings communicated architects' themes using the sun for lighting the offices. Carefully placed bricks created a solid foundation meant to last. Craftsmanship vibrated in the solid oak furniture, wooden chairs and sublime tables.

The bars, backed with large mirrors, reflected upon 150 years ago, but showed you your face at this present time. It reminded me of the time I visited the Occidental Hotel in Buffalo, Wyoming. The hotel featured the "Teddy Roosevelt" bedroom. I sat on the bed where he slept. It featured a bordello, saloon, hot tubs, restaurant and shaving salon. Presidents like Woodrow Wilson stayed there along with other notables like Jack London, Buffalo Bill and dozens of other western heroes.

The bartender said, "When you look into that mirror, you're looking in the same mirror that Teddy Roosevelt looked into when he stayed here. He walked these floors in his time."

"Gees, Louise," I said. "It doesn't get much better than this."

We rolled eastward out of Waitsburg with smiles on our faces. Great breakfast, beautiful town and stunning statues. We followed the same route run by stage coaches in the 1800's. Muddy roads, wheel tracks rutted into the clay and dust penetrated every lung of every person on those stages. Hard livin'!

We again pedaled our bikes under hundreds of towering, white, wind turbines slashing at the blue sky. We pedaled through more wheat fields, hay and lavender patches. Endless flowers delighted us. As usual, hawks soared on the updrafts above us. When you ride so slowly through such beauty, it soaks into your soul. It smooths the rough edges of our high-speed society. It calms your mind. Like Gerry said, "Riding a bicycle is the best way to see the world."

As we rolled past a week in the saddle, our legs adapted to the eight hours of pounding the pedals. Even at our advanced ages, our bodies responded to the muscular demands placed upon our legs. While following the Columbia, we continued climbing from sea level to 1,000, 2,000 and 3,000 feet into the Cascade Mountains. We rode our bikes through the volcanic "Ring of Fire" known by locals because Mt. St. Helens blew her top in 1980. While riding through Oregon and Washington, Mount Hood, Mount Rainier, Mount Baker and other volcanic peaks pierced the sky with their sharp snow-capped summits.

We enjoyed an uneventful day until we rolled into Pomeroy, Washington, yet another town right out of the 1800's. A stately courthouse stood at the center of the village. An old wooden school house grabbed our eyes with its simplicity. Two story farm houses stood up while old barns showed their simple construction that lasted 150 years.

A farmer directed us to the fairground and museum. He treated us to one of the most magnificent farm-tractor-equipment collections in the state. Old John Deere, Allis-Chalmers, Ford and other tractors dotted the huge warehouse-museum. It featured buggies, combines with 33 horses pulling them, old cars and tools that needed explaining because we had no idea about their use.

After hot showers, we enjoyed our picnic tables, journal writing and a peaceful evening of fellowship.

Next morning, we packed it up, pedaled into town for breakfast, and got down the road.

We enjoyed a great feeling heading down the highway with a full belly, fresh water bottles, plenty of trail mix and the blue sky overhead. We continued our journey along the wide expanse of the Columbia River. Not far along the way, we stopped at a rest area to meet a couple who had paddled their kayaks from St. Louis, Missouri with a finish point of Fort Clatsop, Oregon.

They paddled into a very slow adventure, and hard core. They portaged great distances over land. I don't mind saying that they exhibited true grit, determination and gumption.

We followed the Columbia River along the valley with high, brown cliffs above us most of the time. Huge erosion channels created incredible rock formations. While it's easy to "get used to" the magnificent scenery and maybe take it for granted, it permeates a cyclist's spirit. For starters, you're traveling at 12 miles per hour. It not only opens your eyes to such beauty, it causes you to gulp huge drafts of energy into your being. Many a time while touring through such beauty, I mutter, "I must be the luckiest man on Earth."

We rolled into Clarkston, Washington on the edge of the Snake River that led into Lewiston, Idaho. In this modern world, we enjoy boundary markers, state borders and cities for supply stops. Can you imagine the men on the Lewis & Clark journey wondering where the heck they might be and what about their next meal?

Anybody remember when Evil Knievel attempted to jump his motorcycle over the Snake River from one cliff side to the other? His dare-devil stunt, fueled by alcohol and by a man not quite right in the head, became the stuff of legends. Pretty much a stupid legend, but perhaps no different than Billy the Kid and the Hole in the Wall Gang. When you think of Butch Cassidy and the Sundance Kid, all those characters lived wild and crazy lives—many times by the seat of their pants. Yes, we see them as handsome heroes in the movies with Paul Newman, Robert Redford, Brad Pitt and Bradley Cooper, but in reality, they lived hard, gritty, tough lives.

Staying on Route 12, we headed along the Clearwater River. It's still as crystal clear today as when Lewis & Clark paddled their canoes down it in 1805. So clear, the rocks sparkle off the bottom of the river. Trees grow down to the river's edge on both sides. Elegantly magnificent!

We pitched tents at an old gold mining encampment they called Camp Myrtle.

Henry David Thoreau wrote, "We need the tonic of the wildness— to wade sometimes in marshes where the bittern and meadow-hen lurk, and hear the booming of the snipe; to smell the whispering sedge where only some wilder and more solitary fowl builds her nest, and the mink crawls with its belly close to the ground. At the same time that we are earnest to explore and learn all things, we require that all things be mysterious and unexplorable, that land and sea be infinitely wild, unsurveyed and unfathomed by us because unfathomable. We can never get enough of nature. We must be refreshed by the sight of its inexhaustible vigor, vast and titanic features, the sea-coast with its wrecks, the wilderness with its living and its decaying trees, the thunder-cloud, and the rain which lasts three weeks and produces freshets. We need to witness our own limits transgressed and some life pasturing freely where we may never wander."

(Robert and Frank changing a flat tire.)

CHAPTER 10

Why do You Like to Ride a Bicycle Long Distances?

"Long-distance touring cyclists pedal all over the planet without causing any environmental stress to Mother Nature. Therefore, the cyclist becomes an intricate part of the natural world. Not only that, he or she shares a magical connection that transcends the mechanized world. Rather than riding in a vehicle, the cyclist rides 'with' his traveling companion. The bike and the cyclist become a dance. Every cell in a cyclist's body charges around feeling that it conquered the world. You might call it "pedaling bliss" or for lack of another word, the transcendent joy of being alive." FHW

"Why do you ride those overloaded bikes?" asked a tourist at one of our rest stops.

"Man, that's easy," said Gerry. "Because it's fun!"

"I love the freedom," said Frank.

"It calms my mind," said Robert.

"I love the adventure," said Don. "But if you have a couple hours, I could explain it further."

I've asked myself that same question often during my life on the road on a fully-loaded touring bike. What the heck caused me to ride a bicycle over long distances? I remember my first tour in 1975—strangers made wild and crazy comments. They expressed their astonishment about anyone who would attempt such an arduous journey on a bicycle.

"Are you crazy or just plain nuts?" one guy said. "You're actually going to ride that bike from the Pacific to the Atlantic?"

"You are insane," one college coed said to me on the Big Sur. "You're nuts, just nuts! You need to get a life!"

Let's face it, riding a loaded touring bike in the rain makes me miserable. I endure it. I remember in the Amazon Jungle in Brazil; it rained three hours every day. My panniers suffered mold and mildew. The rain soaked my shoes. It felt terrible riding in thick humidity making me sweat myself to death. My two buddies cursed the clouds and everything else along the route.

Riding across hot, dry deserts causes sweat that leads to grimy skin, dirty clothing and endless thirst. Riding across Australia's Outback makes a cyclist go crazy with the endless desert day after day. And your only companions? Those God-forsaken, demonic bush flies that crawl into every orifice of your body! You can't kill them and you can't escape them. And the heat, 120-degree F. days, suffocates you like a dry sauna. Or, try riding in the Atacama Desert of Chile, the driest in the world! Every day, all you see—sand from horizon to horizon. You're riding through a movie of sand that never ends. It's a friggin' nightmare come to life—and I chose to be in that movie. Am I that nuts?

And riding in the mountains—up and down, down and up, grinding for hours up a 12,000-foot pass—gees, it burns my thighs, wears me out and takes forever to reach the pass. It takes hours to summit a pass, and a few minutes to coast down the other side. The Swiss Alps? Gees, Louise, you climb and climb and climb. And, those 15,500-foot passes in the Andes, in the snow, why in the heck did I think that was a barrel of laughs? What's up with that?

Usually, I make 50 to 60 miles a day. A car covers that distance in one hour. What does that mean in terms of efficiency, miles covered, and energy expended? A motorist can see the entire 48 states in the United States in four weeks in a car. I can barely make it half way across the country on a bicycle in four weeks.

What's the pull here? What's my idea of fun on a bike tour? Why do I put myself through so much physical, mental and emotional anguish? Do I have any good reasons? Hopefully, you're receiving those reasons during this ride across America.

From Myrtle to Kamiah, we climbed, descended and powered our way through wilderness along the Clearwater River. It featured huge stretches of wild river, birds, hawks and deer. At one point, we spotted a bald eagle flying along the river on his dinner patrol. Suddenly, he swooped down onto surface of the river.

"Look at that," Don said, pointing. "He's going for a fish…oops he missed it."

"Gees, he just nicked the water, but came up empty handed," I said. "That is too cool. Are we living inside a nature movie or what?!"

"It doesn't get any better than this," Don said.

In Kamiah, we stopped for dinner at the Pizza Factory. A pizza never tastes so good as when you devour one at the end of the day. Each bite offers a taste sensation extraordinaire.

As usual, Don asked the local boy, "You know where we might camp around here?"

"Just before the bridge, turn right into a park," he said. "You can camp under the pavilion near the river. There's hoses for you or you can jump in the river."

Fat and happy, we pedaled down to the bridge where we turned into the park. We found the grandstand to be perfect and took baths in the river. The Clearwater River lives up to its name. It runs as clear as glass, so much so, you can see the rocks 10 feet under the surface and 150 feet across.

That night, we slept like the rocks in the river with the gentle current carrying a tune of its own.

Next morning, we pedaled back to the grocery store for supplies. Don lost his glasses, so I backtracked to the campsite area to find them between the pavilion and wood braces. He bought a securing necklace to hold them around his neck. As we age, it's easy to forget things. Best to keep them tied to us and/or always stick them in a pocket with a zipper.

The one thing I've found during any tour: always keep your personal items in your hand or zipped in a pocket. Never set them down, because you will absent-mindedly walk away.

We rode into the early morning with happy hearts and high expectations. Route 12 showed the usual "Lewis & Clark" trail sign with the explorers pointing the way.

We pedaled along the Middle Fork of the Clearwater River. Each curving mile offered geese, diving ducks, wood peckers and hummingbirds buzzing about the flower patches. Deer popped in and out of the trees along the river. At one point, we saw a beaver methodically swimming toward his dwelling along the wood-line. A king fisher sat on a branch above the water, preening himself. Life prospers along a river.

Mountain man John Muir wrote, "How many hearts with warm red blood in them are beating under cover of the woods, and how many teeth, beaks and eyes are shining! A multitude of animal people, intimately related us, but of whose lives we know almost nothing, are as busy about their own affairs as we are about ours."

As to why we bicycle long distances, Bob Johannes, 72, out of Winter Park, Colorado, a veteran cyclist coast-to-coast across America, Ragbrai and Norway, gave his account:

On a Saturday and 10 years old, I found myself riding on Olivia Avenue in Ann Arbor, Michigan. I couldn't remember making the turn from Granger headed to my friend's house. I braked, stopping in the middle of the street, my mind bathed in total puzzlement. That was my first bicycle 'wow' moment. Sixty plus years later I tour in search of wow, wonder and amazement. Here are a few of my, "Oh, my God!" moments.

1. Preparing to ride the coast of Norway I climbed to the top of Colorado's Berthoud Pass. Wanting to memorize the moment I asked a visiting tourist to take my picture. He and his two buddies were pilots from Norwegian Airlines in Denver for their annual training. How does that happen? They were right to advise taking good rain gear to Norway where, "There is no bad weather just bad choice of clothing."

2. It takes us two grueling days to ride Tioga Pass road in early May from the floor of Yosemite National Park to the Tioga Gas Mart in Lee Vinning, California. Standing in the food line, our buddy that we left behind in Yosemite said, "Hi." How did he climb Tioga Pass road in one day at 80 grueling miles of climbing and descending? Why does this gas mart have a band outside and such great food inside? Why are people so friendly they are offering us free beer?

3. Sitting by a fire-ring of camp stoves at the end of the day and being offered hot hard-boiled eggs and hot chocolate. Best road food ever!

4. A buddy and I left Panamint Springs, California at sea level in the Mojave Desert. We started grinding up an 18 mile long pass road at 8 and 10 percent grade. We're barely moving, eyeglasses fogged out from evaporated head sweat, sun blazing down and temperature hovering north of 100. After six hours, we reached the top of the pass at 5,000 feet. Death Valley stretched before us. Ahead a car pulls off the road. The father and son duo got out to await our arrival. After greetings, dad reached into the trunk while saying, "I think you two might like these," as he handed each of us an ice cold can of San Pellegrino Limonata. We looked from one to one another and in an instant, started laughing.

I enjoy fretting over my packing list; using the kitchen scale in search of the elusive wasted quarter ounce, searching for lower granny gears to make climbing bearable as I age. But the reason I go through all this is the ride to the next unforeseen moment of wonderment.

(Frank Cauthorn riding lead across the Northern Great Plains.)

CHAPTER 11

A Point on the Compass of Happiness

"Have you ever wondered what causes all this beauty we cycle through? What creates the energy of trees, rocks and that eternal ocean off to our right as we pedal south? What makes that sky above us change so often in only an hour? What creates the magnificent rivers we cross on our two-wheeled journey? Do you contemplate deeply while pedaling your bicycle? Do you feel the essence of the creative energy of the universe pulsing through everything around you? It streams through rocks, plants, birds, wind, fire, water and animals. It vibrates through you. On your bicycle, you recognize an enormous amount of energy coursing through all the cells in your body because you travel down the road with a happy heart and a big smile on your face as you dance with the universe." FHW

What thrills you as a first-time coast-to-coast touring cyclist? "When I think about our cross country ride this summer," said Don Lindahl.

"It brings a flood of emotion, mostly good with a few exceptions, most notably something we couldn't control, the weather.

"The best part of the memories of our bicycle ride across America stems from the sense of adventure, with every day bringing something new and different. When that sun came up, we were up and on our way toward a new adventure every day. We knew that there would be some good and bad to this trek but the good far outweighed the bad in every sense. Our bodies, minds, and spirits were so energized that we had to learn to manage them so as to not let fatigue in any aspect overcome us.

"We learned to pace ourselves in so many ways because this was not a sprint but a marathon that would call on the best of all of our faculties to endure and succeed in our goal of riding over 4000 miles in two and a half months of constantly changing landscape. In addition, it was important to be careful to respect our compadres and encourage and assist in any way possible to maintain the integrity of the "team". We were all for one and one for all in this adventure. And, to the extent we took sage advice from more experienced riders, we were successful reaching our destination each day

"As I reminisce and ruminate about the accomplishment of this epic journey, I am overwhelmed with the great memories of people we met and joy we shared at many points along the way. We stayed in numerous homes as welcome guests of our new-found friends each day. It is a testament to the wonderful character of so many who live in this great country of ours. I also greatly enjoyed riding with Gerry and Frank. They were two very solid boys who were always in good spirits and ready for the new day with something cheery and positive to add to the conversation. This adventure shall forever be part of one of the most memorable summers of my 70 years on this planet."

With the afternoon sun bearing down on us, the heat caused us to stop at a sandy beach along the Middle Fork of the Clearwater River. The sun warmed the water to a delightful 70 degrees. We jumped in with great enthusiasm.

"Hey," Don said. "Let's ride that current through the rapids 50 yards up river. Should be a lot of fun."

"Let's do it," I said. "Come on Gerry!"

"I can't swim very well," he said.

"Hell," I said. "If you start drowning, I'll swim out to save you. Come on, this will be a blast."

We made our way up the shoreline covered with rocks and sand. At one point the rocks jutted out into the river to give us a launching spot.

"Yeehaw!" I yelled as I jumped into the current.

Gerry and Don jumped seconds later. The raging water quickly grabbed us for a high-speed ride through the rapids. It swept us 50 yards downstream as we whooped and hollered with glee.

"Let's do it again!" yelled Don.

Like a bunch of kids, we climbed back over the rocky shoreline to our launch site—and leaped into the current for the ride. Two hours later, we decided we better ride to find a campsite.

That's what I love about spontaneous adventure. Travel when you want, stop when you like, take pictures, write notes, sing songs, eat to your heart's content, and go with the flow of life.

Later in the afternoon, we reached Lowell to stop at a restaurant stocked with pies. A man named Jack from Chicago stopped, too. He rode from the east coast toward the west coast. He bought everyone a piece of huckleberry pie. We listened as he told us about the high points of his ride.

"Man, thanks," said Gerry.

"You guys have a great ride," said Jack.

We pedaled happily along the river until 7:00 p.m., where we found a hidden cove with a path down to the water. We pitched our tents, took baths, cooked dinner and sat by the campfire. Gerry got out his guitar for our usual songfest. "If I could save time in a bottle...." by Jim Croce. Gerry sang it with mystical perfection. We sat back in our own worlds as he soothed our souls. I think all of us shed a tear.

As with all songs from the 60's, each of us carried our own memories of those tumultuous years.

Don spoke about how his wife left him with a three and five-year-old. He moved out to Colorado to start a new life. He worked full time while being a single dad.

"I miss my kids," he said, teary-eyed. "They grew up too fast. They flew the coop and now my daughter lives in California and my son lives in Mongolia. I'm so proud of them, but they live a long way away. And, there's nothing I can do about it."

Every guy on this ride suffered divorce. Each of us experienced heart ache of losing a best friend, being betrayed or lied to by bosses or friends, and most of us felt disappointments in our lives about something or other.

If I would have only done this or chose that or.…

We all remembered Kent State, Walter Cronkite, Vietnam, peace marches in Chicago, Detroit, New York City and Washington, DC. We remembered Simon and Garfunkel with "Bridge Over Troubled Waters." We remembered ty-dyed T-shirts, Motown, peace signs and draft cards. We smoked dope, got high or got drunk. "Hell no! We won't go!" Each of us lost a friend in Vietnam or saw him wounded for life. I lost my college floor mate. He got drafted. He wrote me from Fort Benning, Fort Polk and from rice paddies in the Mekong Delta. Then he got killed!

Lord, I never cried so much.

Who doesn't remember the Righteous Brothers', "Unchained Melody."

If you're reading this account, you're probably a baby boomer, so you carry your own story. At this late time of your life, you give more thanks and appreciation that you made it this far.

In the morning, we pedaled along a new tributary called the Lochsa River. The same clear water ran over rocks. Same deep wilderness— the same as when Lewis & Clark paddled their dugout canoes down this very river 214 years ago. At noon, we once again jumped into the river for refreshment. Later, we jumped off a log stuck over the river to humorous color commentary by Don.

"Here we have the contestants in the Bicycle Log Jumping Contest of the modern-day Lewis & Clark expedition," said Don. "Here's Gerry with his graceful approach to the end of the log, and, er, oops, folks, poor Gerry slipped and fell into the water with an awkward backflip having more to do with slipping on the wet wood than a more disciplined approach...."

Late in the day, we left the river when the road began climbing toward LoLo Pass at 5,200 feet. Just before some serious climbing, we stopped to camp at the Lochsa Lodge, a beautiful cathedral ceiling dining room with cabins all around it. Formerly a hunting and fishing lodge, today, it serves all clientele. And, it offers cyclists free showers and camping.

Of course, we ordered fantastic food and drinks that cost a fortune. All the while, we talked with other cyclists and guests from around the country.

Sometimes, on a bicycle tour, the forces of the universe line up to give you a sense of joy, a sense of bliss and a sense of aliveness unknown to the work-a-day world. You pedal through lush green forests too quiet to be real. You leap into cool waters churned by the rocks along the riverbed. You witness the universe playing its own tune and inviting you to its dance.

Are you looking at the animals or are they looking at you with the same wonder? You glance at the heavens for a brilliant visual feast. Billowing clouds skid across the azure sky garnished with flashing white horsetails. You taste your food with a sense of devouring delight. Why does an orange taste like heaven on your tongue? How does it feel to be out-of-your-mind happy? It feels good from your nose to your toes.

You bask in the fellowship of your friends. It feels joyful to sit at the table with a giant feast before you. Has a pizza ever tasted so good at the end of the day? In those moments, satori decorates your soul. It carries you into physical, mental and emotional ecstasy. That night, as you climb into your tent, the full moon enhances the smile in your heart.

(Gerry and Don devouring their freshly baked pies compliments of a fellow cyclists as they pedaled toward LoLo Pass along the Middle Fork of the Clearwater River.)

CHAPTER 12

Wow! What a ride!

*"If you want to get more out of life, you must lose your inclination for monotonous security and adopt a helter-skelter style of life that will at first appear to be crazy. But once you become accustomed to such a life you will see its full meaning and its incredible beauty. In short, get out of Doldrums City and hit the road. I guarantee you will be very glad you did. You had a wonderful chance on your drive back to see one of the greatest sights on earth, the Grand Canyon, something every American should see at least once in his or her life. But for some reason incomprehensible to me, you wanted nothing but to bolt for home as quickly as possible, right back to the same situation which you see day after day after day. I fear you will follow this same inclination in the future and thus fail to discover all the wonderful things that God has placed around us to discover."
Jon Krakauer, Into Thin Air*

That quote reminded me of the guy who walked up to me at Multnomah Falls. He decided at that moment to live his dream because he saw others living their dreams. You want to live wild, free and ornery? Solution: go do it! At the end, you slide into home base, all scratched up, banged up and busted up from living a rambunctious life. Finishing up in a rocking chair with a remote stuck to your hand doesn't quite cut it for those of us who love the raw taste of life.

In the morning, at Lochsa Lodge Restaurant, we ordered pancakes with all the trimmings.

"Holy mother of Jiminy Cricket," said Don, when the waitperson served up his pancakes. "How am I supposed to eat those skyscrapers?"

Before him, pancakes measuring nearly a foot across and an inch thick awaited his ravenous appetite.

"Dudes," Don said. "Can somebody help me with this? These pancakes are bigger than my head."

"Don't mind if I do," said Frank and Robert, forking the cakes.

Around us, the inside dining hall offered 50-foot-high cathedral ceilings. Elegant round tables dotted the dining room. A buffet offered scrambled eggs, hash browns, pancakes, biscuits and gravy, orange juice, coffee, fruit salad and omelets.

On every wall, elk, moose, deer, beaver, fox, antelope, owls and hawks looked down at us. For whatever reason, humans like to immortalize the animals they kill. Trophies! Personally, I like to shoot pictures and leave everything alive in my wake.

We struggled to consume the pancakes. Nonetheless, we loaded up knowing we faced 5,200-foot LoLo Pass. Fortunately, Lewis & Clark borrowed horses to transport them over the pass. Once they reached the Lochsa River, they gave them back to the Indians for safe keeping until they returned. At that point, they cut out and burned out more canoes for the long journey to the Pacific. As usual, we saw signs showing where they camped along the journey.

With full bellies, we started to climb. Grinding away in Granny gear makes for a slow start to the morning. At six percent grade, we usually make four miles per hour. First, sweat beads up on our arms and legs. Next, it drips off our noses. Our pits get wet and rivulets drain down the backs of our spines. The road wound around the side of the mountain like a giant anaconda snake. It became a continuous dance with the mountain, a slow dance, very slow.

The mountain maintains your attention with each pedal stroke, heaving lungs and muscle contractions throughout your body. After 100 yards or 200 yards or 300 yards, you stop to swig great gulps of water. You feel hunger quickly, so you gobble a banana. In essence, you consume life. You chew into it with a ravenous appetite for living. At the same time, life consumes you. Life envelopes you in its arms, heart and soul. As life dances with you, something occurs that gives you the heart and spirit to continue up that mountain grade.

Describing that "occurrence" might best be the term "satori", or "perfect moment." You don't think about the past or future. You live in the perfection of the moment. You also gain a rhythm corresponding to the pedal strokes. You power down with your quads and let up on the back side. The other quad muscles take the power stroke and then, give it up to the other leg. You do it enough and a certain trance carries you to the top.

Another factor happens on a climb. At first, you look at the tops of the mountains. You climb through steep valleys. Deciduous trees like aspen flourish at lower levels along with mountain flowers brandishing their colors along the road. Higher up, you start looking down into the valleys while the mountain tops draw ever closer. You watch aspen leaves below you flutter in the breezes. At higher altitudes, pines dominate. Pretty soon, you're even with the mountain peaks.

Several hours later, you see the road cut over the top of the pass. You reach the top. It's a moment of serendipity. You called on all your muscles, lungs and heart to take you to the top. All of a sudden, you feel your pedals relaxing beneath your feet as you gain level ground. Your mind relaxes, and your body surrenders to the inescapable joy of gravity taking over your flight.

At the top, a Lewis & Clark National Park ranger station welcomed us with video films of the journey over LoLo Pass. They offered hot chocolate for refreshments and dozens of books for sale. Huge wooden signs outside the station gave visitors an idea of their journey through the mountains.

"Amazingly," Frank said. "It's just as wild today up here as it was 200 years ago."

"Did you read in the station where Clark lost a horse that was carrying his desk on the horse's back?" Gerry said. "Why would they force a horse to carry such a non-essential?"

"Go figure," said Don.

"Hey, there's the "Welcome to Montana" state line sign," I said. "Let's get some pictures."

We stood in front of the "Montana" sign. Three states down and ten more before the Atlantic Ocean.

For the next 27 miles, we soared down the mountain like eagles on the wind. The road curved with steep mountain ramparts on one side and steep canyon drop-offs on the other. Waterfalls and rivers began their descent as we dropped away from the pass. Two other cyclists waved as they cranked up the pass east to west. They biked upward; we soared downward. We enjoyed such an elegant, graceful flight through time and space on our way to Missoula, Montana.

"One final paragraph of advice: do not burn yourselves out. Be as I am a reluctant enthusiast.... a part-time crusader, a half-hearted fanatic. Save the other half of yourselves and your lives for pleasure and adventure. It is not enough to fight for the land; it is even more important to enjoy it. While you can. While it's still here. So, get out there and hunt and fish and mess around with your friends, ramble out yonder and explore the forests, climb the mountains, bag the peaks, run the rivers, breathe deep of that yet sweet and lucid air, sit quietly for a while and contemplate the precious stillness, the lovely, mysterious, and awesome space. Enjoy yourselves, keep your brain in your head and your head firmly attached to the body, the body active and alive, and I promise you this much; I promise you this one sweet victory over our enemies, over those desk-bound men and women with their hearts in a safe deposit box, and their eyes hypnotized by desk calculators. I promise you this; You will outlive the bastards." – **Edward Abbey**

(Frosty, Robert, Gerry and Don at LoLo's Pass
and Montana state line at 5,200 feet.)

CHAPTER 13

Moment at a Convenience Store Known as The Incident

"What does a man or woman need - really need? A few pounds of food each day, heat and shelter, six feet to lie down in - and some form of working activity that will yield a sense of accomplishment. That's all - in the material sense, and we know it. But we are brainwashed by our economic system until we end up in a tomb beneath a pyramid of time payments, mortgages, preposterous gadgetry, playthings that divert our attention for the sheer idiocy of the charade. The years thunder by, the dreams of youth grow dim where they lie caked in dust on the shelves of patience. Before we know it, the tomb is sealed. Where, then, lies the answer? In choice, which shall it be: bankruptcy of purse or bankruptcy of life?" — *Sterling Hayden, Wanderer*

Frank Cauthorn said: I love riding my bicycle. I have four bikes and they are all for different types of riding. I love riding my bike for the sense of freedom it gives me. I can ride down the street or across the country. I love fresh air and the morning dew when pushing out of where I camped the previous night.

I love riding my bike and discovering and seeing things that people speeding by at 65 mph never notice. The slower pace of bicycle touring has a calming "peaceful easy feeling." I love riding my bicycle to the world's natural wonders and experiencing the beauty of mountains, lakes, rivers, hot springs, beaches.

I love riding my bike to historical places and soaking in the knowledge of the place. I love riding my bike through rain, cold, heat, hills, bugs and all the other stuff that happens on a bike ride. I always say what doesn't kill ya' makes a great story later. But maybe the best thing about bike riding is the personal relationships I make along the way. I met Frosty and Don touring through Yellowstone National Park. I have met so many wonderful people riding bikes.

Touring cyclists almost always stop and exchange stories and information about where to stay the night or some cool place to see. Trail angels are a daily experience. I discover the good in humanity. Bicycle touring simplifies life down to the basics of food, riding, and sleep. Oh, and I must laugh a lot. Part of Frank's Hierarchy of Needs! I love bicycle touring because it's an environmentally friendly and a very inexpensive way to travel. I love riding my bike because it makes my mind and body strong, with a large dose of happiness.

We pedaled right up to the doorstep of Adventure Cycling Headquarters in Missoula, the bicycle center of the world, and the famous Adventure Cycling Magazine. Editor Alex Strickland and his crew of jolly bicyclists publish maps, run tours and provide cyclists with the latest information on all aspects of touring. They offer pictures, ice cream and soda pop for everyone. And, we bought some touring maps for the Northern Tier of the American ride. The mapping team offered many different maps showing sights, campgrounds, and best routes.

My new friend Gerry owns the bragging rights as the first and only Irishman to ever ride coast-to-coast across America east to west and west to east. His first ride included Ireland's famous cyclist, Dave Turner, author, entrepreneur and international perfume expert. I met those two men in 2013 on the Continental Divide. We shared a week of laughter while pedaling up and down the Continental Divide. Of course, I invited them on this ride. Gerry took me up on the offer.

Missoula, Montana proved itself the most elegant, delightful and bicycle friendly city in the Rockies. The city featured beautiful sculptures, garden paths by the river, classic 1850 buildings, organic food stores, movie stars like Andie McDowell, and down-home friendly folks. It's a regular Norman Rockwell city.

In Missoula, Frank gave us all a fond farewell as he needed to take care of family business in California. It's a sad moment to lose a touring brother. On such a journey, you actually fall in love with the folks on the ride with you. It's a brother and sisterhood family. Frank, probably the strongest cyclist on the trip, and a Hawaii Ironman triathlete, always showed great energy, encouragement and friendship along our route. We felt that profound sadness at his leaving the tour. It's like losing an intricate piece out of your favorite puzzle. The picture can't be completed. In this case, the moving part, a fellow cyclist, could no longer ride with us.

"Dude," Don said. "Thanks for the memories."

"Frank," said Gerry. "Loved every minute of the ride with you."

"Thank you, Frank," said Robert.

"Glad we met in Yellowstone," I said. "And so glad you made the trip. We'll hook up again."

"You got that right," said Frank.

We rolled out of Missoula on Route 200 toward Great Falls, Montana. Immediately, we hooked up with the Blackfoot River. It wound in and around the mountains on a lazy summer day. Green wilderness and colorful flowers stretched along the highway. Blue sky above and smooth pavement under our tires created the perfect ride.

We pedaled with easy delight the entire day. At one point, a motorcycle guy stopped and asked us to look for his cell phone that fell out of his pocket somewhere along the route for the next 50 miles. He gave me his card. All of us glanced along the shoulder and into the grass for the rest of the day, but found nothing. I phoned him a day later with the sad news.

Late in the day, we crossed over a beautiful river until we reached a fork in the road.

"That northbound road Route 83 goes to Glacier National Park," said Don. "We go straight on Route 200. But let's get some food at the corner convenience store."

We pulled into a gas stop with automatic pumping systems. But the store sign read: closed for repairs. Out front, several benches offered us a respite along with some porta-toilets.

Robert decided to go back to the river to find a campsite. "I'll see you guys back at the river."

This event shall be forever known as "The Incident" by Don Lindahl:

Frosty, Don, Robert and Gerry had been riding for the better part of the day in the wild and woolies of eastern Montana. In the popular vernacular, we were in BF Egypt and had no idea how much longer it would take to escape the incessant hills and head winds of that desolate part of the world.

We headed east on Highway 200 about three weeks into our journey across the country. We noted on the map that there was a "T" in the road with Route 83 heading north to Glacier Nation Park. We felt some level of confidence that there would be a gas station along with some food. As it turned out, we found a gas station with a good-sized store but unfortunately the store was closed for renovation for that day and it was only possible to buy gas.

In short, there was no one there to help us with food and sustenance. We were SOL. The station featured an air pump, so we checked our tires and sat down on the bench outside the store to commiserate and lament our bad luck. Gerry, being a good Irishman, and I had a habit of finding a beer or two each evening to slake our thirst from a long day of riding, so it was doubly disappointing. Frosty had been a reluctant participant in our daily refreshments but on this occasion, we were able to coax him into joining us.

The one thing that offered some encouragement was the fact that vehicles were regularly showing up to purchase fuel. Once they got their tanks filled, they headed out on their merry way. As resourceful souls tend toward creative thinking on occasion, it occurred to Gerry and me that we just might find one of these wandering souls who would sell us a libation.

So, we carefully chose our prey and pounced...though very judiciously, after sizing up each driver for our potential prize...... booze......of any kind. I ventured off our comfortable bench, headed out to the gas pump and described my sorry plight. Here I stood, a tired and hungry senior citizen cyclist with no way to obtain anything to drink due to the closure of the store. I offered some money but to my surprise, no need.

We soon honed our story and our sad condition was conveyed with ever more fervor. I am sure our dramatic presentation had nothing to do with the fact that we had been successful with about a half dozen "helpful" passing patrons of the pump. The first rancher in a pickup truck gave us beer. Another woman in a motorhome offered some kind of pink Smirnoff lemonade. Another lady brought us some VERY powerful glug from a motorhome from Arkansas. By this time, we were trying to decide whether we could ride the bikes any further or pitch the tents in the parking lot. Frosty, who rarely drinks a drop for his entire life, was so giddy that we thought about bedding down right there in the on the benches.

Laughter and joking never came any easier than it did that evening. In a way, we felt glad about the store closure. We created a memory that will stay with us forever. Fortunately, we found our way to a small campground and slept off the joy of that evening.

Frosty's version of "The Incident."

As we sat on the benches of a closed convenience store one night, the following escapade took place:

"I need a beer," said Don.

"Why don't you beg for a few beers from people stopping for gas?" I said.

"Not a bad idea," said Don.

A big motorhome stopped at the pumps. A very attractive lady pumped fuel into the big rig.

"Ma'am," said Don. "Could you by chance help a poor Irishman with a bottle of beer or two. I would gladly pay you for your troubles."

"My dear man," she said. "My husband can help you."

Moments later, three beers appeared out of the motorhome.

"Thank you so much," said Don. "What's the damage?"

"Hey," he said. "You guys inspired us to try something like you're doing. It's on us. Thanks."

They drove off. We sipped our brews. Fifteen minutes later, another motorhome pulled into the pumps.

"Sir, do you have any spare beers?" said Gerry, getting into the act.

"How about some screwdrivers?" the man's wife said.

Minutes later, we sipped on screwdrivers, replete with chips. No cost!

Another fifteen minutes passed, and another motorhome stopped.

"Would you have any beers for three tired senior citizen cyclists," said Gerry.

"Would you like some hard lemonade?" a woman asked. "I've got some potato salad, and bagels, too."

She stepped over with three ice cold hard lemonades, potato salad and bagels.

"On the house," she said.

By this time, please remember that I am not a drinker. I maybe drink six beers, one at a time, during the entire year, and only at a friend's house on a hot day. I actually don't know what beers and liquor do to you.

Suddenly, I felt giddy sitting there on that bench with a beer-drinking Irishman. I mean, Gerry can drink an eight-pack in a heartbeat. Don not far behind him. They laughed at everything. I started laughing at every comment or nothing at all. Suddenly, everything they said sounded funny. I laughed until my eyelids curled up on my eyelashes.

As we sat there, the whole world felt funny, if not hilarious. My two buddies laughed and talked about everything and nothing. I said one thing and they started laughing. They said something and I started laughing. I laughed so hard my face cracked with pain. My guts tightened up.

As you can imagine, after a long day in the saddle, I felt thirsty as a horse coming in from the plains. If someone offered me liquid, I drank it. But at that moment, I realized I exceeded my pay grade as to alcohol.

"That's it, boys," I said, laughing. "I'm done with this alcoholic, bagel, chips party."

"What's wrong with you?" asked Don. "Can't you hold your liquor?"

"I can't tell if I can hold it or not, but I'm heading for camp," I said.

With that, I got up, walked over to my bike, slung my foot over the top tube and pedaled off toward the river. The sun shone its final pink tracers racing across the sky. Trees on both sides of the highway seemed to wave at me in the breeze. A hawk soared overhead, lit by the last rays of the sun. As I approached the bridge, I heard the rippling waters pressing over the rocks. I took a right onto a gravel road. Within a minute, I found Robert asleep by the rippling stream with a small waterfall near his tent. He picked a peaceful, perfect spot to camp.

In minutes, I pitched my tent. Don and Gerry followed and pitched their tents near the water. With one last look at the sky, I dove into my sleeping bag. I looked out the flap to see the night stars twinkling all over the Milky Way. The Big Dipper popped into the sky with Orion showing itself. Scorpio, Cancer and Pisces jumped out of the star pattern. The North Star shone brightly. Saturn offered a night light in the sky. The moon, well, the "Old Man in the Moon" has lighted my life's path over the decades. He's like an old friend. Good night Don, Gerry, Robert. A day well lived puts a smile on your face during your deep sleep in the arms of the wilderness.

(Our bikes stacked up at the Adventure Cycling
headquarters in Missoula, Montana.)

CHAPTER 14

What explains bicycle adventure?

"When bicycle adventure-touring turns from days into weeks and weeks into months, you turn a corner in your mind, your heart and your spirit. You tap into a wellspring of uninterrupted marvel with the natural world. You push two pedals that give your body renewed energy with every stroke. You see things differently while gaining whole new perspectives. You transform from one person into a whole new individual every day. Ironically, no psychologist can figure it out. But you know! The energy of the universe charges through every cell in your body to create pure magic." FHW

Long distance touring bicyclists pedal a fine line between a call from the roguish angels of hell to a state of angelic bliss in the far reaches of their minds. Why would a sane person choose sore arms, numb hands, painful butt, crotch rot, rubbed raw thighs and dehydration of every cell of his or her body, day after day?

Why oh why, pray tell, would someone set off on a piece of steel frame, connected to two wheels, wrapped in rubber tires—to discover his or her life's calling? For many, why such a quest to catapult themselves into another dimension not attempted by 99.9 percent of humanity?

Why pedal one's life away from comfort, security and constancy—into the realm of the unknown, danger and insecurity?

My friend Tom Middaugh, veteran touring rider, said, "We like to believe there's magic. The reality of it is right in front of our faces. It's right inside us. It's our heart, it's our desire. It's passion I want to learn about myself. I want to learn how far I can go. It's about challenge. We naturally want to strive for something. The rawest form of striving is surviving."

One other aspect comes to mind: we remain animals, animals that think. No matter how civilized, we harbor primal lusts, savage instincts and survival genes. Rarely do those aspects of our lives become tested in 21st century modern day existence.

On that bike, a 5,000 to 16,000-foot mountain pass lets you know you're alive. That raging hunger drives you to devour your food like a saber tooth tiger. That animal scrounging around outside your tent at night wakes up the beast in you. That pain in your rear-end lets you know the difference between comfort and throbbing agony. As your lips stick to your gums or hang-up on your teeth, you understand the meaning of thirst. Crotch rot challenges your tenacity, yet you pedal through it. That straight-away through the desert tested your endurance to withstand monotony. And, when that rain drenches every inch of your body, you cry out in terse soliloquies of frustrations that make Shakespeare proud.

"To be or not to be…what the hell am I doing in the middle of the Great Plains riding a bicycle?" you mutter to yourself.

And yet, you answer the call of the long-distance bicycle rider. You follow in the same high energy of Thomas Stevens who cycled around the world in 1884-1886. Whatever drove him, drives you. Be thankful. Whatever your father and mother bequeathed to you, that open road pulls at your soul. It freshens your spirit. It drives you higher and farther.

On a bicycle, you "fly" at the "perfect speed" with a comet's tail of memories following you into eternity.

Those moments on your bicycle adventure present you with uncommon experiences that give your life eternal expectation. That's adventure.

We woke up to enchanting mist rising off the waters of the stream where we camped. It mingled with the grass. It slid over the small dam in the river to accent the cascading waters that slipped over the shallow rocks. As the sun rose, the mist created rainbows from all angles over the water. I stood with my camera, "Oh my God, just the right place at the right time and the right luck. Hey Don, are you seeing this wonder?"

"Right on your tail with my camera," said Don. "Can you believe waking up to this magic?"

"Maybe one of the most enchanting campsites I've ever encountered," said Gerry from his tent. "I need to compose a song about this one."

Just then, two mallard ducks skidded into a pool with a few quacks and fluttering feathers.

In his tent, Gerry wrote new music or his memoirs. Robert slept like a log. Before us, the enchanting mist evolved with the rising sun. We stood quietly in the midst of Mother Nature's dreamlike charm.

"Let's pack and find breakfast in the next town," said Robert, crawling out of his sleeping bag.

Within 45 minutes, we headed east on Route 200 again. We grabbed more water at our abandoned convenience store. Soon, we rode our bikes into a fresh new day.

A short 13 miles brought us to Ovando and the Stray Bullet Café. We passed two westbound cyclists, but they didn't want to stop and talk. We waved.

The Stray Bullet Café emerged right out of a western novel. The building dated back into the late 1800's. All wood. Elegant design. We sat at breakfast tables where cowpokes, ranchers and farmers sat for the past 120 years. You might hear spurs jangling if you listened hard enough. In fact, no need, as four of ranchers walked in with spurs jangling.

Back on the road, we rolled up and down hills with mountains on the north and south side of us. Trees, fields, cattle, horses, black birds and hawks! The road presented a ribbon-like quality rippling in the wind. We pedaled along that ribbon in sheer bicycling delight.

Ahead, black plumes of smoke billowed upward into the blue sky.

"Must be a heck of a forest fire up the road," said Don.

"Yup, and we're rolling toward it," said Gerry.

We reached Lincoln, a sleepy, small town thick with tall pines, with the grizzly bear theme everywhere you looked: Grizzly Bear Inn, Grizzly Paw Hardware, Grizzled Café, Sleeping Grizzly Grocery, Bearly Cold Ice Cream Parlor, Roaring Grizzly Campgrounds and more.

At the grocery, Don asked, "You seem to like grizzlies around here, ma'am."

"One walked down the street yesterday," she said. "They own this town. No sense arguing with them."

"Great, and we're camping out with them," Robert said.

"You got that right," she said. "Just keep one eye open and your ears peeled all night…if you hear one of them, hop out of your tent and run for your lives."

"Oh great," I said. "No out running a grizz."

"Yup," she said, matter of fact. "Just hope you can outrun your friends."

We pedaled another ten miles in the late afternoon to find a campsite near the road in some pine trees. In the morning, we faced 5,600 foot Roger's Pass. A wide valley swept away from us. The view: dark green pines surrounding small lakes sprinkled with aspen trees fluttering in the breeze. Aspen means: aspen tremulous or trembling leaves. Farther out, mountain peaks, touched by snowfields, jutted into a pale blue sky.

We crawled into our sleeping bags while looking out over that vast wilderness. To think that those 33 men did the same back in 1805. You must wonder the hardships they endured, but then again, you cannot duplicate the sights, sounds and wilderness they encountered. Here we sit in these tents, seeing and adventuring just like them, in our time. Grizzly bears, yup, all around us. Got to love it! And, keep one eye open and one ear peeled for the sound of a grizz.

"Bears are made of the same dust as we, and breathe the same winds and drink of the same waters. A bear's days are warmed by the sun, his dwellings are over-domed by the same blue sky, and his life turns and ebbs with heart-pulsings like ours, and he was poured from the same First Fountain. And whether he at last goes to our stingy heaven or not, he has terrestrial immortality. His life not long, not short, knows no beginning, no ending. To him life unstinted, unplanned is above the accidents of time, and his years, markless and boundless, equal eternity."
John Muir, 1871

(Bikes stacked up at Roger's Pass.)

CHAPTER 15

A Guitar Player
Sings His Songs

"There is an ecstasy that marks the summit of life, and beyond which life cannot rise. And such is the paradox of living, this ecstasy comes when one is most alive, and it comes as a complete forgetfulness that one is alive. This ecstasy, this forgetfulness of living, comes to the artist, caught up and out of himself in a sheet of flame; it comes to the soldier, war-mad in a stricken field and refusing quarter; and it came to Buck, leading the pack, sounding the old wolf-cry, straining after the food that was alive and that fled swiftly before him through the moonlight." — Jack London, Call of the Wild

"I would rather be ashes than dust! I would rather that my spark should burn out in a brilliant blaze than it should be stifled by dry-rot.

I would rather be a superb meteor, every atom of me in magnificent glow, than a sleepy and permanent planet. The function of man is to live, not to exist. I shall not waste my days trying to prolong them. I shall use my time." — Jack London

Waking up on the side of a mountain makes for an amazing sunrise. At first, the heavens turn from black with stars to pale sky. As the sun crests the mountain peaks, it burns light into the valleys below. This morning, it tipped the tops of the pines, and then, slowly crept over the valley in a wave of light. Once it hit the lake below, the entire surface sparkled into a ga-zillion diamonds.

"Let's git goin'," said Don. "We're burnin' daylight."

"You do know that we've got a big pass to climb," said Gerry.

"So, let's get our butts on the road," said Robert.

After packing, we hit a quiet Route 200 with zero traffic. Nice because that's the way Lewis & Clark enjoyed this journey. Nothing but them, the green and the animals.

"We've got a four-mile climb," I said.

"Piece of cake," said Don.

We began in Granny gear, stayed in Granny gear and ended up in Granny gear. I run a 24-front chain ring to a 34 freewheel. It pretty much allows me to spin and enjoy the ride at four miles per hour. And, I stop to take lots of pictures.

At six percent grade, we pounded up that pass with relative ease in the morning sunshine. Cool temps! We hardly cracked a sweat.

At the top, we enjoyed a magnificent view of the west behind us and the eastern plains before us.

"Sign says 5, 610 feet, Continental Divide," said Gerry. "Should be a nice downhill free ride."

"We're moving out of the mountains," said Don. "I'm sad to see them go."

After several pictures, we launched ourselves onto a six percent, 10-mile-long gravity-powered fun ride. Free and easy. Fun and fabulous. We enjoyed effortless sailing through that mountain air like a Golden

Eagle soaring over his domain. Again, we rolled along curves like ribbons in the wind. We crossed over rivers, rode alongside one stream and enjoyed the endless bouquet of flowers along our route.

Off to our left, we saw huge black plumes of smoke encompassing 125,000 acres of burned forests and plains.

We continued 50 miles before reaching the outskirts of Great Falls, Montana. At the edge of town, we pulled into a "1950's Muscle Car Festival."

"We gotta' stop here boys," Don said. "These are the cars of my youth."

"Mine, too," said Robert.

Rows of '57 Chevy's, Fords, Camaros and Buicks. We stared at a 1934 Ford wagon. They called it a "Woody" in the famous Beach Boys surfer song. GTOs, Malibu's, 1963 Corvette Stingray, 1961 Chevy Impalas. Barracuda, 442, and just about every muscle car ever manufactured made its presence at that car show. Also, they located the car show at a Dairy Queen Brazier to give it that 50's flavor.

Later we pulled into a motel stop to meet my wife Sandi and our friend Cynthia, our trail angels. Everybody took a rest day to relax, take hot showers, eat great food and see local attractions. We visited the Charles Russell Museum, the great Western artist. We visited the Great Falls Lewis & Clark Interpretative Center, which presented movies and artifacts of the expedition of the Corps of Discovery. They built the center on the first of the Great Falls where the expedition dragged the boats up the hills, made wooden wheels, and portaged them 17 miles past all nine falls to move the expedition forward. We're talking HARD work and LONG days of heavy labor.

When you see the movies showing their "true grit", it becomes apparent how gargantuan a task they experienced. After having ridden nearly 1,000 miles of their route on my bicycle, I flat-out don't know how they survived the merciless hardships and death at their door daily.

Two days later, we all gathered in town, grabbed a bunch of food stuffs, and biked eastward on Route 87. We blew down the road onto wide open plains with a 30 mile per hour tailwind.

I hate headwinds. At the same time, tailwinds make me so happy, every cell in my body 'thrills' to the energy of the wind at my back. Those tailwinds give every muscle in my body a gift of love. Tailwinds sooth my soul. Tailwinds, yes, God sends tailwinds to make every man and woman on a bicycle happy beyond imagination. Those winds blew us into Stanford, Montana, where we asked the grocery clerk where we could camp.

"You can pitch your tents in the city park," she said. "And, there's a pool and showers along with picnic tables."

"Wahoo!" Don yelled.

We found the camp, along with Cynthia and Sandi. After showers and food, Gerry brought out his trusty guitar to strum a few songs. I don't mind telling you that when he starts playing, the magic flows out of the chambers of his heart, his mind, his emotions, and his spirit. He picked out several songs for the ladies. They swooned. I'm sure many women over the years have fallen in love with Gerry and his guitar. He's got a magic voice that lifted our spirits every night he played. He sang:

"Time in A Bottle" by Jim Croce

If I could save time in a bottle,
The first thing that I'd like to do;
Is to save every day till eternity passes away,
Just to spend them with you.

If I could make days last forever,
If words could make wishes come true;
I'd save every day like a treasure and then,
Again, I would spend them with you.

"It's a magical thing, the guitar. It allows you to be the whole band in one, to play rhythm and melody, sing over the top. And as an instrument for solos, you can bend notes, draw emotional content out of tiny movements, vibratos and tonal things which even a piano can't do." David Gilmour

(It's a 1934 Ford wagon and they call it a "Woody"
made famous by the Beach Boys.)

CHAPTER 16

Raging Wildfire
Across Montana

*"Adventure creates unique "moments" for your heart, mind and body.
You never forget the time when you slogged through a downpour
along Oregon's coast. You remember that tornado funnel as you
pedaled across Oklahoma. That special campfire under 14,000-
foot peaks in Colorado stands out with shooting stars placing an
exclamation point on your day. You remember that trip across Death
Valley where you drank four gallons of water in one day, but
never peed once. That night of slumber beneath the 2,500-year-old
Redwood giants touched your spirit beyond your imagination. That
night in the Sierras where Canadian geese dropped out of the sky for
a final landing pad on the glass-still lake before you. Other ducks
created V-wakes trailing behind them while diving ducks created
circles. With that magical scene, your campfire's embers enchanted
you. While those moments abound on a bicycle adventure, the new*

day beckons you onward, not to tarry with yesterday—and, for you, another possibility for a unique 'moment' that will live in your body, mind and heart for the rest of your life." FHW

One aspect of bicycle travel: you never know what you're going to run into from day to day. You never know what's around the next bend in the road. You have no idea what's at the top of yonder pass or at the bottom of that river valley. You cannot fathom where you're going to camp. How far does that desert stretch in front of you? Will that rain cloud up ahead dump all over you, or will your prayer be answered, "Dear God, let it pass before I get there."

You face surprises from people, animals and weather. You meet endless challenges that toughen you up or break you down into tears. Headwinds kick the crap out of your body and mind. Tailwinds thrust you into ecstasy. Hunger pulls at your stomach like a wild animal and dehydration makes you thirsty enough to drink out of a horse tank. You sweat like a pig in a rainstorm and you smell like the southbound end of a northbound goat after three days with no shower.

Of course, if you ride in one of those group tours, none of this applies. A sag wagon aids hapless riders who wrote a check that their bodies can't cash. Group tours provide wonderful bottled mineral water at all times. It bubbles! You enjoy a shower every night. Someone starts a campfire to make you all warm and cozy. A sumptuous breakfast awaits you in the morning while you dine on the finest salads at lunch—also ham, cheese, lettuce, pickles, tomatoes and mayonnaise sandwiches. Dinner, oh wow, a five-course extravaganza created by a five-star chef. Endless chocolate chip cookies, cakes and pies! And, for the men, scantily clad trail angels drop organic grapes into your mouths as you sit under an exotic Amazon princess fanning you. Plus, wine and beer! And, somebody washes the dishes while you sit by the campfire penning the next All-American Bicycle Adventure Book.

On tour by myself, I never know where I'm going to camp. It might be behind a bunch of porta-potties, a church or an abandoned radio station building. I've slept in cow-pie infested pastures and junk yards.

Several cemeteries! You can only imagine the interesting horror dreams I've suffered. I pitch my own tent, cook up some rice and beans for the tenth night in a row, and maybe I remembered to bring some bagels. I chomp on bananas and a bag of peanuts. I gather my own firewood, light the fire, and sit on a rock writing my next best-selling bicycle book. I stink like a skunk and my socks, oh God, my socks smell worse than moldy Gouda cheese.

After writing the first paragraph, maybe I should seriously start thinking about a life of ease with a group tour. This hardcore cycling life ain't all it's cracked up to be! On second thought, it's the only way I roll.

We pedaled through elegant mountain terrain that spread out behind us. The temps reached 100 as we pedaled through Winnet, Montana, a town with endless junked cars, junk yards and generally ugly as hell. Hard to figure out why people live amongst debris and broken-down trailer homes. They could, at least pick up the trash and haul the junked cars to a central landfill. Is it IQ? Is it low sociological upbringing? How can they stand it? It's a peculiar trait of some farmers and others to create junkyards in their own yards.

We ate at the Little Montana Truck Stop featuring the "Greatest Cookies in the Universe."

"I'll take four," I said.

"Okay guys, take a bite out of the universe."

After eating a huge bowl of oatmeal, I groaned at the pancakes and toast everyone tried to play off on me.

A local artist painted unicorn pictures, framed them and charged $750.00 per painting. Very ambitious for such terrible renditions!

We listened to farmers and ranchers talk in cowboy slang about the fires ahead. "Why, he was so skinny, he had to jump around in the shower to get wet," said one old rancher describing the skinniness of one of his cowpunchers.

"Ya'll are looking at 260,000 acres of burned prairie," one said. "The road's open but could close at any time. You're headin' into some really nasty country."

We pedaled into the heat. After two hours, a small town appeared up ahead. I thought, watermelon! We stopped at a local grocery where they offered big fat watermelons on ice. I bought one for the whole group. We sat in the store cutting it up and feasting on cold, sweet, delicious, juicy, red watermelon.

"I don't care what anybody says about you, Frosty," said Gerry. "You're okay in my book."

"Here, here," everyone yelled.

We jumped back on Route 200E and continued for a total of 53 miles toward Mosby. To the north, black plumes of smoke covered the sky. Enormous black swaths of land stood stark against the brown grasslands and few trees. Thankfully, it all blew north with a south wind blowing across the road.

The night before, Robert did a superb job patching his collapsing sidewalls on his ragged tires, and he repaired the tubes shot with holes. His tires and tubes resembled Swiss cheese. About ten miles before Mosby, Montana, Robert's chain broke.

"Dude," said Don. "You need to hitchhike a passing pickup truck for a ride. You'll easily get into Mosby before we get there."

"Never expected my chain to break," said Robert.

"We'll see you in Mosby," Gerry said.

At that point, Robert faced 300 miles to the nearest bike shop. As we departed, an old farmer in a pickup stopped to transport Robert to Mosby and a camper-van campsite. We rolled into camp an hour later. Almost beyond amazing, we all ordered pizza and beers to celebrate the ending of a great day, and Robert's getting a ride. Still, to the north, black plumes of smoke commanded the skies.

Great pizza, great drinks and warm showers! In the morning, we faced 50 miles of blackened prairie.

Robert and the old man, Blake, took off in his truck. The old guy transported Robert over 300 miles to the east. That put Robert six days ahead of us. Since he faced a wedding date with one of his kids, Robert kept riding into Michigan. We never saw him again for the rest of the trip. He texted the wedding exceeded his wildest dreams.

We broke camp at 8:00 a.m. with clear skies, but quickly, the winds blew southward, and with them, smoke.

"Dudes," I said. "We gotta' get down the road before they close it again."

"Right behind you," said Gerry.

We pedaled into a thick, nauseous, bank of smoke. Fire touched down on the road in several places. Firefighters looked at us as if we were from another planet. We climbed and descended through smoke. All around us, black fire-burned grasses and fence lines. Cows wandered around looking for food and water. They bawled their lungs out. In several places, we viewed dead carcasses of animals that didn't run fast enough from the flames. We looked 360 degrees around us to see everything blackened by fire.

We rolled along with our lungs feeling like we chain-smoked cigarettes for six hours. Finally, in the mid-afternoon, we pedaled out of the smoke to see a huge firefighting staging area with men and trucks, resembling a small army.

We headed eastward to find a camp spot somewhere on the prairie. We felt weary, smoked to death, dirty and ready for a shower.

It's like Forrest Gump said, "Life is like a box of chocolates." Your life resembles that simile. You put yourself out there into the universe to see what happens. Mostly positive! You learn from the good and otherwise. That's what creates the experiences that build your dynamics as a person. It makes for an interesting journey.

For certain, I'm glad we rode through that prairie fire. It offered a lesson: life isn't always a box of chocolates. Sometimes you must struggle through the smoke and flames to discover yourself. In this case, we didn't shy away from adventure, we pedaled into it with intrepid hearts.

(Gerry and Don riding through the smoke of a Montana wildfire that burned over 260,000 acres of prairie. We saw burned carcasses of cows, antelope and birds. We pedaled through flames that burned right down to the road. We inhaled smoke for six hours before pedaling out of the fires.)

CHAPTER 17

Nothing is Fair in the Great Sweep of History

"Tentative efforts lead to tentative outcomes. Therefore, give yourself fully to your endeavors. Decide to construct your character through excellent actions and determine to pay the price of a worthy goal. The trials you encounter will introduce you to your strengths. Remain steadfast. And, one day you will build something that endures; something worth of your potential." Epictetus, Roman philosopher

In the morning, open prairie awaited us on our long journey across the Northern Great Plains. We faced enormous distances with little more than prairie dogs, antelope and deer for our companions. Crows flew across the highway in front of us. Sparrows chirped along with red wing black birds. At intervals, marsh hawks soared overhead in search of a mouse or rabbit. Barbed wire fence lines presented us with a corridor across Montana.

After asking around town, we found some teens who gave us directions to the city park with water and bathrooms. We camped out in the park under a pavilion. So nice to take a shower under a spigot. We talked, wrote and spent the rest of the day quietly, until a blazing sunset blew the socks off of us at twilight.

Around the campfire, we talked about the challenging cycling of the day.

Don asked me, "Who is the craziest person you've met while on tour?"

"Man," I said. "I could write a book about the many characters I've met. But I guess one in particular stands out on a tour in New England: People along the journey make bicycle adventure special. They approach me at every stop. Curious and full of questions, they make my day with their homespun hospitality. They advise me about local events and interesting places to visit. I'm invited into their homes for a hot shower and dinner. But it's those rare, eccentric characters that cross my path that intrigue my imagination."

Most of us enjoy a chance to fill up our lives with seventy to eighty years of living, and we can use them as we see fit. Some of us do it in highly imaginative ways. For a few, travel is the ultimate freedom of expression. It brings the unknown into focus.

Traveling east toward Vermont on Route 373, I stood on the dock waiting for the ferry to take me across Lake Champlain. Spring colors decorated upstate New York. The boat wasn't due for another hour, so I pedaled around the parking lot until I found a spot to write in my journal. I'm usually the center of attention with flags flying and a dozen bananas hanging off my rear packs. Not that day! Another traveler commanded MY attention.

In the corner of the parking lot, a buckboard wagon right out of a John Wayne movie stood silently in the shade. It featured a shortened harness on the front, along with a blue and white cotton surrey top. Pots and pans hung from the sides along with a fold-out table and bench. It sported four heavy rubber-covered large spoked wheels. A series of plastic covered news clips were tacked to the sides of the frame. The most curious aspect of this contraption wasn't evident until I rode closer.

A gold-trimmed black coffin comprised the main compartment of the wagon. The news clips featured a dozen languages.

Off to the side stood a man who looked to be in his mid-sixties. Long silver hair flowed from under his cap and he sported a goatee. His eyes matched the sky. He bantered with some Aussie tourists about some experiences in Australia.

I looked at the news clips until I found one in English from the London Times. This guy had traveled through 85 countries on five continents. They called him "The Coffin Man."

Backing up, I grabbed my camera for a shot.

"Hold it, sonny," he said. "Please read my sign before you take a picture."

"What sign?" I asked.

"Right here," he said, pointing.

I moved closer to the rear of the wagon. It read, "If you are going to take a photograph, I ask that you donate $1.00 and I will stand in the picture with you. This is the way I make a living for my travels."

"Sounds fair enough to me," I said, handing him a buck.

After the shot, I asked him how long and why he had been traveling with his buckboard.

"It's been twenty years this coming May," he said, stroking his goatee. "It dawned on me when I was forty-five that my life was passing me by. My kids were grown, and my wife died of breast cancer. I was broke, but in good health. I worked a year to save up money to travel around the world. Within ten months, I was broke again. But by that time, I had the travel bug. I figured I wanted to see every place on this planet before my time is up. I itched to get back on the road. That's when I thought up this idea to make money while I traveled. It's the cheapest way to go, and I make a decent buck along the way."

"Where's the horse?" I asked.

"You're looking at him," he said, slapping his sinewy thighs.

"You pull that wagon?!" I gasped. "How do you get it up the mountains?"

"I've cut out any extra weight, so it's pretty light," he said. "Here, you can pick up a corner to see how light it is. You'll be surprised."

I laid my bike down and picked up a corner of the wagon. It weighed about 200 pounds, maybe less, but I could see that a strong person could pull it up a mountain grade.

"So where do you sleep?" I asked.

"Sonny, it doesn't take an Einstein to figure that one out," he said.

I looked up at the wagon.

"No," I said. "In the coffin?"

"Yes," he said.

"Hey, you guys! My wife and I would like to take a picture of you two crazy people," a tourist said. "After that, we'd like to take you out to lunch, if you don't mind."

"You don't have any idea how much I eat," I told him.

"No, you won't believe how much I eat," the Coffin Man said.

The couple snapped our pictures before taking us to lunch. They asked more questions than a reporter. They were fascinated by our different modes of travel. Late into the afternoon, we finished a long discussion of world politics, people and countries around the world. I had missed the ferry, but could catch it in the morning.

I asked the Coffin Man what was one of his favorite adventures in his travels.

"It's hard to pick out one favorite moment out of hundreds," he said. "But once, I was caught in a monsoon rain on a muddy road in India. I had given up hope of getting out of there for the rest of the day. As luck would have it, three guys rode by on their own modes of transportation."

"What was that?" I asked.

"Elephants," he said. "They hitched up one of those beasts with a rope to my wagon, and then motioned me to hop on board with them. Hell, I didn't know how to get up on one of those things, so they motioned me to the front of the beast. I stood there when the elephant got up close to me and rolled out its tusk in front of my foot. I stepped into his curled snout, and that elephant hoisted me up to his back. It was the most exciting elevator ride to the second floor of any building I've ever taken."

That night, we camped together. We both agreed that we had an incurable love for travel. I crawled into my tent and looked out the netting to see the Coffin Man climbing into his bed. I don't mind saying that it was a strange feeling watching this man who was so much alive, and who was living such an incredible life—casually climb into his coffin and close the lid behind him.

Our discussions that day excited my passions for travel, and reminded me of a piece written by John Steinbeck in his book, **Travels with Charley**.

"When I was very young and the urge to be someplace else was on me, I was assured by mature people that maturity would cure this itch. When years described me as mature, the remedy prescribed was middle age. In middle age, I was assured that greater age would calm my fever and now that I am fifty-eight perhaps senility will do the job. Nothing has worked. Four hoarse blasts of a ship's whistle still raise the hair on my neck and set my feet to tapping. The sound of a jet, an engine warming up, even the clopping of shod hooves on pavement brings on the ancient shudder, the dry mouth and vacant eye, the hot palms and the churn of stomach high up under the rib cage...I fear the disease is incurable."

Laying there on my back, with a million stars twinkling in the night sky, I smiled realizing that the adventure travel 'bug' or if you want to call it a 'disease', flowed through every cell in my body.

"That's a hell of a story," said Gerry. "You're crazy like a fox for your world travels."

"Damn," said Don. "Hope I meet a character like that."

"You will if you keep riding," I said.

Next day, we pedaled twenty miles of up and down until we hit a pass. Then, downhill and 15 miles of flats all the way to Glen Dive. We again camped in a city park. The next day, we faced North Dakota.

In the morning, Gerry said, "The distant horizon calls us."

"And distant it is," said Don.

On the road, we met an MIT professor from Boston who saved three years to bicycle from Boston to Seattle. He bragged that he pedaled 110 to 120 miles a day. I quietly thought, 'You cycling fool; slow down and smell the flowers, talk to people, rest and enjoy the ride'. I've done 120-mile days. They bust your butt and burn up your legs. You don't do anything but pedal. No fun! Hard work! No let up! No pictures! No spontaneous conversations! But you know, to each his or her own.

A second couple, from Minneapolis, Minnesota bicycled toward Astoria, Oregon, dragging 50 pounds of dog and trailer.

I can't figure out why anyone would haul that much extra weight. The dog sits in the trailer all day and the guy must burden his legs with the 50 pounds of extra weight. Again, to each his or her own.

That night, we camped in a town park, but a chemical mosquito fogger whipped around with a massive cloud of some horrible chemical to kill the skitters. Of course, that fog kills the birds, the insects, the angleworms, the grubs, the squirrels and in the end, and the ground water suffers poisoning. Humans never learn. Rachel Carson's **Silent Spring** documented all the deleterious consequences of chemicals upon the land. Instead, humans keep spraying Round Up, DDT and 70,000 other chemicals into the air, land and water 24/7 all these decades later. Makes me sick! Thankfully, the wind blew away from us, so we didn't inhale it all night long.

On Route I-94, we pushed against 30 mph headwinds all day. Endless misery, slow going, pounding the pedals, aching feet, and a sense of futility. Nine hours in the saddle and only 40 miles! Gees, Louise! Up and down hills, gusts up to 50 mph.

The two most challenging aspects of a long-distance touring rider: headwinds and rain. One causes misery while the other causes more misery. Take your pick. Which do you choose? Answer: you don't enjoy a choice. Either one kicks your butt and brooks no complaints. No whining, crying, hurt feelings, bleating, bellyaching, grumbling or grouchiness. If you want to cry; go back to the soothing arms of your mother. You live in a cyclist's world on this day; grit your teeth, gnash your gumption and get yourself down that road. Or, you could call it a day, park your bike, pitch your tent and read a book. We'll send a nurse-maid every hour to check on you.

Today, we busted our rear-ends and racked our quads by struggling against "Boreas", which means: unruly north wind. I gnashed my teeth with a tenacity given to me by my father. He said, "Son, if you put yourself into any situation in the wilderness, you get your butt in gear and make the best of it. You conquer it with a steadfast resolve to finish what you started. No one will ever feel sorry for you, and never feel sorry for yourself. There's always a lesson. Learn it and move on."

Thanks, dad. He gave me resolve like few others. Actually, riding with Gerry and Don becomes a brotherhood of road warriors. We all shared that same tenacity. Those boys powered into this day just like me. They gritted their teeth and busted into Boreas with a sense of resolve. Yes, it sucks! And no, it won't quit if you start crying.

So, what do you do? You hammer those pedals and get down the road.

We felt so worn out at the end of the day, we booked a motel on the state line in Wibeaux, Montana. A hot shower and how meal never tasted so good!

The ride from Wibeaux to Dickinson, North Dakota found us buffeted by side winds from the north until we hit the North Dakota and the National Grasslands. The land slowly morphed into dramatically painted canyons, layered and colorful, with pink, bronze, topaz, golden, tan and white sand.

We stopped for lunch in Theodore Roosevelt National Park. The entire town near the park geared toward jeep adventures, mountain biking and hiking. Really nice, and pretty much out in the middle of nowhere.

That night, we stayed at another motel. We met three elderly Indian ladies at the café who talked about the Mandan Indians who helped the Lewis & Clark Expedition to stay alive in North Dakota. Unfortunately, the U.S. Government sent troops to conquer them and place them in Internment Camps only 50 years later. The ladies talked about visiting "Crying Hill" where the squaws waited for their men to come home from fighting the pale faces. When they couldn't see their warriors, they knew they had died, so they wept at the loss of their men.

When you look at the bloody map of history, the black man became free by a half-million white men dying in the Civil War. As to the Indian Wars, the red man lost his life, his tribe, his language, his religion, his ethos and his freedom. To this day, the red man suffers on reservations with booze and the hopelessness of lost culture and very little ability to work into the white man's society. I've read the three big ones: **Bury My Heart at Wounded Knee, Sand Creek Massacre, Trail of Tears.**

Those books made me sad and disheartened. To this day, it's still heartbraking, if not depressing. I've visited "Custer's Last Stand" where 250 cavalry troops lost their lives to 3,000 Indians, the last victory for the red man. Here we ride on that same "trail of tears" for the Mandan's. The one thing I've learned in life: nothing is fair in the great sweep of history.

"On the mainland of America, the Wampanoags of Massasoit and King Philip had vanished, along with the Chesapeakes, the Chickahominys, and the Potomacs of the great Powhatan confederacy. Scattered or reduced to remnants were the Pequots, Montauks, Nanticokes. Machapungas, Catawbas, Cheraws, Miamis, Hurons, Eries, Mohawks, Senecas, and Mohegans. Only Uncas was remembered. Their musical names remained forever fixed on the American land, but their bones were forgotten in a thousand burned villages or lost in forests fast disappearing before the axes of twenty million invaders. Already the once sweet-watered streams, most of which bore Indian names, were clouded with silt and the wastes of man; the very earth was being ravaged and squandered. To the Indians it seemed that these Europeans hated everything in nature—the living forests and their birds and beasts, the grassy glades, the water, the soil, and the air itself." **Bury My Heart at Wounded Knee**

(Every American sings "Home, home on the range;
where the deer and the antelope play....")

CHAPTER 18

Surging of Life Through
a Cyclist's Body

"He was mastered by the sheer surging of life, the tidal wave of being, the perfect joy of each separate muscle, joint, and sinew in that it was everything that was not death, that it was aglow and rampant, expressing itself in movement, flying exultantly under the stars."

— Jack London, Call of the Wild

That same "surging of life" or "tidal wave of being" expresses itself in the long-distance bicycle explorer. You press into those pedals each morning with your muscles, joints and sinew raging toward the emerging day. You feel aglow and ravenous for adventure. You express all of it in the movement of your bike flying down the road like a horse galloping across the plains. A certain rhythm flows into your muscles as you pedal toward the horizon. Your body beads up in sweat while droplets drip from your nose. Your thighs rise and fall with a renewed energy for a new day. John Wayne said, "Tomorrow (today) is the most important thing in life. It comes into us at midnight very clean. It's perfect when it arrives, and it puts itself in our hands. It hopes we've learned something from yesterday."

From New Salem to Steel, North Dakota, we rode a long day at 65 miles. Flat, wheat fields and croplands. In all this land of nothingness, a tack punctured my front tire.

These days, I enjoy an I-Pod to listen to music during such mundane, long distances. I rock on with Willie Nelson, Waylon Jennings, Elvis, Roy Orbison, Garth Brooks, Dean Martin, Karen Carpenter, Whitney Houston, Adele, Aretha Franklin, the Beatles and Frank Sinatra. I like to hear the lyrics of the songs. Does my love of their music make me an old guy? You betcha'!

At the same time, I watch the horizon, birds on fences, coyotes trotting and antelope grazing in the fields. I pedal into a cadence that allows my entire body to run through that "surging with life" aspect of living.

From Steel to Jamestown, I suffered another flat tire. Gerry and Don hammered down the highway. That night, we stopped in town to present Don with a strawberry milk shake for a pre-birthday gift treat as he turned 70 on the adventure. Next day, we treated him to breakfast. And, Gerry bought a watermelon that he carried on his pack to eat for a birthday celebration on the highway.

While in Jamestown, I met up with my old college roommate John Stchur and his wife Sharon. We enjoyed several hours of conversation and remembrances of our college years. John became a teacher and later, after retiring, he became a successful novelist in the style of Stephen King. Later than that, he turned into a romance author. Sharon became a fantastic artist. They visited, and she painted in the Yellowstone area. After breakfast, they hit the road and we did, too.

Down the highway that day, we sang "Happy Birthday" to Don, and on the overpass, we celebrated Don by devouring that watermelon. For sure, we acted like a bunch of kids eating, laughing and making fun of 70 years of living on this planet. Can't think of a better way to celebrate your birthday than riding into a great bicycle adventure with your old friends, gray beards and all.

We arrived in Medina, near Chase Lake, where we stopped for lunch at a broken-down café. Near the place, President Teddy Roosevelt created a bird sanctuary named White Pelicans Park.

Which brings me to this point; Teddy Roosevelt lived a remarkably adventurous life. Jack London explored the planet on the high seas and traveled to the Yukon. Jim Bridger, the mountain man, carved his name into the history books. So did Amelia Earhart, Nellie Bly and Gertrude Bell. Today, Jane Hunt explores the West with her magnificent paintings. Jaclyn Tanemura packs her way around Canada and beyond. Rayne Grein rock climbs and conquers mountains.

The point I am making: most people dream of living an epic adventure or great moments in their lives, but most take the easy route. They ride a tour bus or guided safari or carnival cruise ship. Very little effort expended! Sure, such adventures create memories. At the same time, there's no need to dig deep or opportunity to expend oneself.

If you're a baby boomer from 50, 60 to 75, and you like to ride a bicycle, but you haven't lived an epic moment such as a coast-to-coast ride—you might consider it. I've lived endless adventures on this planet in my 72 years, and I can say that bicycle touring captures my/your "edge of wonder" while being kind to your body. Even if you have steel knees and plastic hips sockets, you can pedal a bike. If you can't pedal up mountain passes, you can choose flat routes as noted in Adventure Cycling. You can also buy an electric assist bicycle that gives you a boost on climbs.

Give such an adventure some thought, and then, make plans, and take action. I guarantee you this: the rest of your life will point to that one extraordinary event where you pedaled your bicycle across an entire continent. And when you take your last breath, you will enjoy a shit-eating-grin on your face and in your heart, that you lived an epic adventure in your life.

The old ladies in the café talked about how the town suffered a slow death. Buildings suffered abandonment and people moved away. Once all the old people died, the entire town faced certain death. All of the women remained single from divorces or their husbands died.

"There's not enough men in this town," one said. "And, I can't marry Jesus! I don't know what to do."

We nearly fell out of our chairs laughing at that surprise statement.

We rolled through more wheat fields, bales of hay and plenty of ducks in numerous lakes along the route. We rolled another 20 miles to find a camp site.

On our way across North Dakota, we crossed over the Missouri River, the exact spot where Lewis & Clark Corps of Discovery paddled their boats on their epic adventure. We rolled 1,500 miles on the same route where they explored. Our journey gave me a funny feeling in my guts to comprehend their gargantuan journey without any idea of the outcome. We knew where we were going and when we would arrive at a known destination. We bid those explorers a fine farewell as we crossed over the river and continued on our way eastward. That was their time; this is ours.

In the morning, we rode past more lakes, more birds, more pelicans and rolling hills with incessant 18-wheelers blowing by us like tornadoes.

We reached Fargo, North Dakota to visit the Great Northern Bicycle Shop located in an old train station. Best shop I've seen anywhere! Don bought new tires for his bike.

Outside the store, we met Rory riding from the East Coast to the West Coast and back again to the East Coast all in one summer. That's nearly 8,000 miles. He complained about his painful butt with a Brooks Saddle. Some people love them, and some can't handle the pain. Everybody eventually finds a saddle that works for them.

We asked about a campsite at the bike shop. They said the park would make a good spot. But when we arrived, a lady told us the police would toss us out in the middle of the night.

We rode along the street until we asked a woman about a camp spot. She said there was one 10 miles away, but we could stay in her yard and use her bathroom. At that moment, the rains opened up out of the sky and drenched us. First rain of the trip!

"You can camp under the porch," she said. "My husband Chris likes to ride and my son Mathew."

"You dear lady," Don said. "Are a trail angel."

Within a half hour, we pitched the tents up for a night under a porch with a wild-eyed teenager hanging on every word of our adventure. Great kid, and great parents. Plus, we felt their act of kindness to take three strangers into their home, bathroom and porch for the night.

At the end of each bicycle adventure, I keep addresses of each person who treated us so well. I send them a packet of my "Spirit of Adventure" greeting cards in thanks for their kindness.

In the morning, they left for work and we rode our bikes into Minnesota. We decided to make it a rest day by grabbing a motel and lounging for the rest of the day in luxury. Hot tub, showers and pool! We met several other cyclists. One couple from Germany pedaled around the world.

You might enjoy this humorous comment by cyclist Scott Martin: On Valentine's Day, I'll present my beloved with a shiny bauble I bought from our favorite store. Next, I'll take my honey out for a sunset cruise, maybe to the spot where we first got acquainted. Later, back home, I'll give my baby a bath. Then I'll gently dry my sweetie and turn out the lights…I'm talking, of course, about my bike…I humbly submit that my bike and I make a better team than most relationships I've seen… Your bicycle invigorates you, strengthens you, relaxes you, lets you vent your frustrations without interrupting, nodding off or making judgments. Your bicycle helps you meet other people. Your bicycle always goes where you want to go. And if you buy your bicycle a box of chocolates for Valentine's Day, you get to eat them all.

(Don and Gerry at the Minnesota state line.)

CHAPTER 19

Crossing the Mississippi River

"Bicycling...is the nearest approximation I know to the flight of birds. The airplane simply carries a man on its back like an obedient Pegasus; it gives him no wings of his own. There are movements on a bicycle corresponding to almost all the variations in the flight of the larger birds. Plunging free downhill is like a hawk swooping. On the level stretches you may pedal with a steady rhythm like a heron flapping; or you may, like a hawk, alternate rapid pedaling with gliding. If you want to test the force and direction of the wind, there is no better way than to circle, banked inward, like a turkey vulture. When you have the wind against you, headway is best made by yawing or wavering, like a crow flying upwind. I have climbed a steep hill by circling or spiraling, rising each time on the upturn with the momentum of the downturn, like any soaring bird. I have shot in and out of stalled traffic like a goshawk through the woods." Louis J Halle, birdwatcher and cyclist

The next day, on Route 10, we pedaled 90 miles with ten-mile-per-hour tailwinds and flat land. Northern Minnesota featured huge maple and oak trees, along with pine and poplar that dominated the landscape. Instead of viewing the road all the way to the horizon, the trees created a green tunnel that limited our view. We camped near a cornfield.

The road led through huge trees, speckled with farmland, and back to trees. We rode through Park City, to Walker and on to Remer.

We saw our first loons today. That haunting cry from the loons harkened back to wilder times in our country's history. About a decade ago, a friend and I canoed the Boundary Waters in Eli, Minnesota. We camped out at night on islands in the lakes. The loons called out at twilight. One evening, I paddled the canoe right into the middle of six loons, not 20 feet off my bow. They played a game where the one loon dove down and the rest scattered, something like hide and seek. Once the diving loon popped up, he flew to catch another loon and tag him. Then, that loon was "it" and the game started all over again.

Their "game-playing" showed me that animals entertain themselves just like humans.

We arrived in Remer to camp in front of a motel for five bucks. We weren't too excited about camping in the wilds with a report that some black bear attacked a camper in his tent in the middle of the night.

As we waited for a shower in the motel TV room, a guy walked in to rent a room.

"We're filled up," the attractive blond said.

"Dang!" he said. "When I was younger, and this happened, I'd go to the nearest bar and find the fattest chick in the place and go home with her. But those days are gone."

The host lady laughed, and I laughed so hard, I almost cracked my jaw. A good laugh meant a good night's sleep. I took a shower, but as I walked out to the front desk, the lady asked, "Do you have any interesting stories to tell from your bicycle travels?"

"Oh, probably a dozen or more," I said.

"Could you tell me one," she asked. "I've always wondered why so many cyclists ride across the country and what they experience."

"Sure," I said. "This moment happened to me on a bike ride across the Southern Tier of America several years ago. I call it 'Talons from the Sky; Coiled Scales on the Ground.'"

"I'd love to hear it," she said.

"Sure! I headed eastbound across southern California with the sun setting low in the sky. My wife and I looked for a campsite in the rocky terrain east of Joshua Tree National Monument."

"We better find a spot soon," Sandi said.

"I'm looking, dear," I said.

Up ahead, we noticed a fluttering hawk, holding his position as the sky effervesced into pink-white thunderheads in the twilight. Very still! Very quiet!

We pedaled the bikes toward the hawk on that lonely highway. The bird continued its fluttering like a helicopter holding position in order to land. We pedaled closer, closer—until we rode up to the perfect camp spot 100 feet off the highway behind some big rocks.

"I'm going to check out that hawk," I told Sandi.

"I'll get the tent set up," she said. "You want pasta for dinner?"

"Sounds great," I said. "I've got Pesto in my pack."

Quietly excited, I crept over several 20-ton rocks on my way to get under the hawk. He kept fluttering until, suddenly, he dove straight down.

I hurried over rocks and dirt until I crept up to where I figured he landed. Before me, not 20 feet away, in an earthen arena surrounded by rocks, the hawk stood in front of a transfixed rattlesnake. The hawk hopped into the air as it dared the rattler to strike. And yes, the rattler complied by lunging at the bird. He missed. Quickly, the snake recoiled into striking position.

The hawk, using his wings and talons, jumped back into the sky toward the head of the snake, toying with him, daring him to strike. The rattler struck again, but the hawk danced out of the way. For the next 10 minutes, the hawk danced into the air toward the rattler, but avoided the snake's deadly fangs.

They pirouetted the dance of life and death. One looked for dinner while the other struggled for life. One dared death while the other lunged for its life.

I crouched in the rocks transfixed with wonder. Sometimes, I cannot help but thank the bicycle gods for their gifts to me as I travel around this planet on Condor, my iron steed. Who could serve up a moment like this? Who could dream it? Who could imagine it?

Before me, the snake struck, and then recoiled. The hawk hopped up to dare the reptile to strike. Each time, the snake grew wearier and more fatigued. Until, as the last rays of the sun slipped below the horizon, the snake made one last strike for its life, but the hawk seized it by the head with his talons. Seconds later, he pecked it on the head until it died in his clutches.

Moments later, the great hawk flapped his mighty wings with the snake securely gripped in his talons. The hawk took to the sky with dinner for his family. One life lost to give life to another. I watched the mighty hawk fly into the sunset for a memory that sticks with me through the years.

This enchanting moment visits me often when I move into Nature. Without a doubt, Condor carries me into exquisite life-moments that render poetic beauty, life and death struggles, mountain heroics and storms that fulfill my spirit.

"Thank you for sharing that incredible moment in your life," she said.

"You're most welcome," I said. "Good night."

"Good night," she said.

In the morning, we headed for Duluth on Lake Superior on Route 200. While we enjoyed fabulous views of that crystal-clear blue water lake, it proved visually distressing to see so many junkyards along the way.

We pedaled along with deep woods on both sides of the road. We kept rolling to Remer to Floodwood and onto Route 333 to Route 2 into Duluth. We rolled through northern Minnesota with good roads, wide shoulders, few cars and a green tunnel garnished with endless flowers of every color of the rainbow. Above the trees, a blue streak of sky. At intervals, cattails lined the lakes with countless waterfowl—geese, cormorants, mallards, loons, grebes and other birds I couldn't name.

Each small town offered glimpses into America's past. Everything on restaurant walls celebrated catching a big fish or killing a deer, moose or elk. T-shirts read, "Go fishing so you won't need a therapist."

Prices for oatmeal breakfasts dropped from $8.00 to $3.95 with toast. Farmers walked into the restaurants with Oshkosh overalls. Pick-up trucks dominated the roads, along with John Deere tractors dragging balers, rakes and combines.

On the road today, we pedaled over the Mississippi River. At that location, it spanned only 20 yards across. I canoed it 20 years ago. As it widens on its way to the Gulf of Mexico, it reaches over a mile across. It starts in Lake Itasca at 6 feet wide and 12 inches deep. It runs 2552 miles to the Gulf with a vertical drop of 1,735 feet. At 1.5 miles per hour, it took six weeks to reach the Gulf. The ghosts of Huck Finn, Tom Sawyer and Jim hunker down in the night mist along the river.

After 70 miles today, we camped at a bar with a fairground behind it. The bartender said, "You can camp at the horse arena to stay away from the traffic noise."

We rode out to the barrel racing and bronc busting area. We settled into nice grass to pitch our tents and used a hose for washing. Porta-toilets and picnic tables made it a great campsite.

The next day, we crossed over a huge bridge from Minnesota to Wisconsin. We enjoyed a grandstand view of Lake Superior, the largest and clearest of the Great Lakes. Lake Superior boasts the largest fresh water lake in the world. It's more like an inland ocean. It wrecked thousands of ships over the centuries, especially the Edmund Fitzgerald, made famous via a song by the minstrel Gordon Lightfoot.

We maneuvered around town until we found a pedestrian section that carried us over the bridge. When you cross over such a magnificent piece of steel and concrete, it takes your imagination for a ride. Millions of tons of concrete, countless tons of steel and humongous numbers of man-hours constructed that bridge. They set concrete pilings into the base of the river to withstand tons of icebound pressures, winds and gales. Back in the 1800's, settlers floated across such rivers with ropes and barges. They took a full day to complete the crossing. For us, a matter of minutes.

Here we come, Wisconsin, the Cheese Head State!

(Old roadhouse signs displayed in front of a business. Since we are a bunch of senior citizens, we remembered most of these signs from our youths. Some companies failed while others prospered.)

CHAPTER 20

Minnesota, Wisconsin, Michigan

"Raw adventure takes guts, gumption and true grit. You choose to get off your rear-end and power your way into the sheer nastiness of life! Yeah, it might be nice one day, and it could be okay another day—but life might throw you a tornado to test your resolve. You must bring your courage to life. You must dig your feet into the day. You must bring your club to the game of life and intend to take charge. You carry your body and mind into unknown danger. At the same time, you marshal all your senses to discover your finest qualities of spirit.

"While the rest of humanity lives from day to day, you relish physical, mental, emotional and spiritual challenges. What is life all about? Read a book by some philosopher to find out? The hell with that! Get your butt out there into the wind, the rain, the

storm, the tempest! Imprint a living book of your experiences into your own mind-body. Take your sheer guts and face the grit of life speeding toward you. Spit into the wind. Just dare it! What's normal? One friend of mine said, "Normal isn't all it's cracked up to be."" FHW

"Become anything but normal," my dad said, "Kick ass and take names later!" Another more euphemistic way of saying it, by Richard Bach, "The perfect speed Jonathan is not the speed of light or speed of a butterfly. The perfect speed is...being there."

So, get out there, whatever you love doing, and rock it. Express yourself in paintings, photographs, playing a guitar under the stars, climbing, cycling, rafting, kayaking, backpacking, skiing and/or whatever pulls at your heartstrings.

Upper Wisconsin proved flat and thick with trees. The fabled Paul Bunyan and Babe the Blue Ox rambled through the area back in the 1800's. Chicago needed lots of trees to build that city. Even today, lumber trucks turn the pavement into wood-chip highway.

Route 2 ran pretty much straight and true across the state. It opened in several places to the pristine waters of Lake Superior. But mostly, trees lined the highway. Flowers garnished both sides of the road up to the tree line.

We reached Ashland to pitch our tents at a campground on the east end of the city. We enjoyed warm showers and washing machines.

In the morning, a spritely 83-year-old man engaged me in conversation. Then, a 73-year-old told me about his new aorta with an aneurism being clipped to save his life. At 50 pounds overweight, it didn't occur to him to eat healthier. Next to him, another man at least 100 pounds overweight, could hardly get out of his chair. Obesity seemed to be a given in the Midwest.

We pedaled 45 miles to Ironwood and on to Bergland another 25 miles. We changed from Route 2 to Route 28. We watched 14 miles of storm clouds gathering before us.

Suddenly, we saw "Welcome to Pure Michigan" on a beautiful sky-blue sign. Again, we met a little old lady at the welcome station who gave us a rendition of her physical ailments. At 4'10" inches, she weighed in at 230 pounds. She suffered from asthma, trouble breathing, constipation, swollen legs, arrhythmia and she consumed $1,600.00 worth of meds a month. I told her about **The Sinatra Solution** for her high blood pressure and arrhythmia. I also said she might consider returning to her old high school weight of 116 pounds. Her age: 52.

In the afternoon, we enjoyed the "sweet spot" of the day where the pedaling felt as easy as a bird flapping its wings. Pedaling became incidental. The energy flowed through every muscle in our bodies. We passed a beaver dam and pond. One lonely beaver cut a V-wake behind him as he cruised to his hut at the far end of the pond. A few hawks circled overhead. A deer leaped across the road in front of me with another two following him.

As the western sky clouded up, large light shafts pierced downward toward the ground. We saw the rain sheeting out of the sky before us.

"We're going to get wet, dudes," I said. "Hey, there's a big house up ahead."

"Let's ask that lady if we can camp in her yard," said Don.

"Not a problem," she said. "Just don't leave a mess."

"We'll leave your yard clean as a whistle in the morning," Gerry said.

We pitched our tents just before a squall of rain dumped all over us. Dry in our tents, we prepared dinner with soup and bagels. As the heavens unleashed their fury, we sat warm and dry.

"Gees oh Pete's" I said. "It's going to rain all night."

"Looks like it," said Don.

We woke up to clear skies. We pedaled five miles to Bergland, Michigan to stop at their only restaurant. We sat down to fish and animals on the walls. Old Formica tables and vinyl chairs awaited us. Old cracked paint on the walls and a tacky ceiling created the perfect ambiance for Northern Michigan hospitality. We encountered lots of old farmers who just shook their heads as to why anyone would ride bicycles across the country.

(Stealth camping in wilderness areas. The cool aspect of
bicycle touring stems from the fact that you can camp at a
moment's notice in just about any location you choose.)

CHAPTER 21

Chasing our Shadows to Germfask

"After an epic moment on your bicycle during a long-distance tour, whether it manifests as two condors gliding down to check you out on the El Camino Highway in Bolivia at 15,000 feet, or riding your bicycle when a family of penguins waddles up to you in Antarctica, or you meet with an emu named George in the Australian Outback, or you strike up a conversation with a man walking across America on his hands—and a hundred other magical moments—you don't want that 'moment' to end. You want to live in it for as long as possible. After riding Big Sur, I didn't want those two days to terminate, but as I stopped at Gorda, California at the end of Big Sur, I knew my 'moment' with that wondrous ride concluded. Yet, I knew that by continuing to pedal my bicycle, I anticipated yet another 'moment' because life always moves forward. Movement constitutes the lifeblood of bicycling. Life moves with you and

opens to you on an adventure. In essence, you live on the creative edge of life. Pedal into it, live it, love it and thank your lucky stars that you ride your two-wheeled iron steed into astounding moments of sheer magic." FHW

On a long-distance bicycle adventure, you ride into different "moments." Some might bring incredible wonder while others may fetch emotional anguish. Some may bring pain. Other moments might bring spiritual contemplation. Some of them may leave you speechless, but all of those moments will bring out the story-teller in you.

On this ride, two times I felt incredible emotional anguish caused by other individuals on the ride. Several times around the campfire, I enjoyed exquisite spiritual bliss. Some of the sunsets and many of the animals heightened my sense of wonder. Quite a number of people delighted my sense of the beauty of humanity.

For whatever reason, sometimes, some individuals like or they can't help creating conflict. They either try to bait me, or they outright need to create tension or arguments. On tour, I am out-of-my-mind-happy daily. I thrill to the open road. Not a care in the world! Total perfect speed of "being there"! And yet, I must deal with people, their foibles and their passions. And they with me. I think I did a good job on this ride. And, I hope others learned their own lessons. If not, the universe will visit them again with the same lessons.

As I write about it later, a trifecta of natural wonders occurred at Niagara Falls. With each "moment", I gain wisdom or a sense of managing my life toward a more positive understanding of the human drama. It plays out in individuals, and finally, it plays out across the planet. I continue to do my part to make my contribution more positive, more knowledgeable and more enlightened.

Under sunny skies, we pedaled eastbound out of Marquette on Route 28. We enjoyed a straight line all the way to Munising. We glimpsed Lake Superior through the trees along the road. The Indians called it Gitchee Gummee made famous by Gordon Lightfoot's song about the ore freighter the "Edmund Fitzgerald" sinking in a nasty storm.

We ate lunch at a family outdoor BBQ. One couple stopped us on the way out of town to press money into Gerry's hand. It's always nice to receive a kind gift from people who support our journey along the way. There's no question they enjoy a sense of contributing to the trek with their gifts. We arrived in Seney near the end of the day to turn south on Route 77. We rode on a glass-smooth highway at twilight.

"Look at our shadows," yelled Don.

"Yeah, they're playing all over the fields," said Gerry.

At first, as the sun began setting, our shadows ranged from 20 to 30 feet, but as the sun set deeper into the horizon, our shadows elongated to 100 feet across the open land to the east as we pedaled south. I grabbed my video camera to take shots of our dancing shadows across the fields. They jumped up, fell short, elongated, danced in the bushes, slammed against trees, fell into the roadside culverts, and acted funny and captivating all at the same time.

That shadow dance must be noted as one of the magical moments on the ride. Don, Gerry and I just happened to be riding at that instant in time for that 'moment' to impact us for our lifetimes. Truly, we enjoyed dancing with life, singing with life and pedaling into a special dream- come-true in our lives.

We stopped at a canoe livery on a river outside of Germfask. It couldn't have been a more perfect spot.

Around the campfire that night, Don told me to tell one of my more interesting bicycle touring stories.

"Which one of a hundred?" I asked.

"Ah, just pick one that pops out," Don said.

"Sure," I said. "As we played with our shadows near dusk today, I'm reminded of a ride across Arizona that blew my mind."

The evening came upon me with no place to camp. On Route 72, near Parker, Arizona, I headed east into the twilight. It had been a blistering hot day and my body felt like a dishrag that had cleaned out a pot of greasy spaghetti and was hung over the top tube to dry. My chances of finding a stream for a bath were next to nothing.

Nonetheless, it had been a good day. Red flowering cacti filled the air with their sweet scent and pink streaks sliced the heavens into sections while lighting up billowing thunderheads that boiled toward the sunlight. Their tails faded into the eastern darkness. Saucer-like clouds skidded across the sky to the south of me.

Nearing Bouse, I stopped at a closed gas station and parked my bike against the side of the cracked, plaster wall of the building.

"Might as well check the spigot to see if I can get a bath," I said, kneeling by the pumps. "I'll be darned! Water."

I grabbed my soap, razor and towel. The water shot out of the faucet full blast. I soaked myself down—clothes and all. After soaping up my jersey, shorts and socks, I shaved my face. As usual, my neck resembled a bloody dogfight after the razor had done its business. No matter what the ads say about shavers, they can rip a man's neck to ribbons. Nevertheless, my body tingled at the newfound clean feeling on my skin. After rinsing away the soap from my shorts and jersey, I stepped into clean clothes. I hung my wet tights, socks and jersey onto the back of my pack for quick drying and loaded my water bottles.

Bouse featured ramshackle buildings on flat desert sands. I cranked into the cool evening air. A mile out of town, I scanned the road for a campsite. My tires made the only sound as stillness crept over the land. A few birds flew over the sagebrush and the thunderheads had darkened with the fading light.

I don't like being on the road at twilight. Too dangerous!

"Come on, where's a place to camp?" I complained out loud. "I'm out in the middle of nowhere, and need to find a place to sleep."

In the distance, not more than a hundred yards, I saw a building. "Bingo!" I said. "That looks like home tonight."

In minutes, I would have my tent set up behind the building and be cooking dinner. This deserted highway meant a quiet night's sleep.

Suddenly, a coyote loped along the road off to my right 30 yards away. He looked intent on something that caught his eye. I pressed harder on the pedals. He continued loping along, not noticing me. He ran ghostlike in the twilight shadows. He was as quiet as the air.

As I followed him, he veered toward the high side of the shoulder near a bush. When he approached it, a jackrabbit shot out of the cover and headed straight down the side of the pavement. The coyote changed from loping gear to Warp Factor two. Every muscle in his body coiled. The stillness was broken by a cloud of dust from his feet and the race was on. The rabbit did a three step hoppity, hoppity, hoppity hop, then ran four strides like a dog, then three more short half steps, and back to running like a dog.

At the same time, the coyote, with his nose cutting into the air like an F-16 jet and his tail streaming behind him, edged closer and closer. About the second the coyote was about to open his mouth and grab the rabbit, the speedster turned on a dime and shot left across the highway in front of me. Mr. Coyote pulled his teeth back into his mouth and executed a 90-degree turn. From a dead stop of zero, the coyote accelerated again to high speed. Again, the rabbit raced ten yards along the highway and did another right turn. Mr. Coyote closed quickly.

On the right side of the road again, the rabbit, followed less than a few steps behind by the coyote, leaped across a shallow culvert. Big mistake! As he sailed over the ditch, the dark figure of the coyote leaped faster and higher through the air, like a heat-seeking missile homing in on its prey. In midair, the coyote's teeth reached down and clamped onto the rabbit. When they fell to earth, the rabbit screamed a death cry. Silence!

When I pedaled up to the spot, I saw the coyote, with the rabbit in his mouth, melt into the darkness.

"Man," said Gerry. "Sure wish I was there to see that one."

"Do you mean if we keep hanging out with you," Don said. "That we'll see something like that?"

"Haven't you already seen some amazing moments on this ride?" I asked.

"Yeah, just about every day," Don Said. "Those moments come in every kind of package, don't they?"

"You got it," I said.

In the morning, we ate breakfast at the only restaurant in town. A wonderful waitress named Maggie told us about how the town received its special name. Back in the 1800's when Chicago burned to the ground, they lumbered the trees in the area and dumped them into the river to travel downstream to Lake Michigan for transport to Chicago. They called the town, "The Dump."

Later, the city fathers sickened at the name, so they took the first letter of the eight men on the city council and renamed the town, "Germfask." We read all their histories and all their names on a small plaque.

Back on the road south, we reached Route 2 heading toward St. Ignace and the five-mile-long Mackinaw Bridge. At that point, we enjoyed Lake Superior, and now, Lake Michigan with Huron, Erie and Ontario yet to go—The Great Lakes.

When we reached St. Ignace, we enjoyed a fantastic meal on the waterfront at the Mackinaw Grill. Very creative chefs!

In the morning, we caught a boat over to Mackinaw Island to the Grand Hotel, famous for its horse-drawn carriages and no motorized vehicles since 1898. Their choice created a feel for living before the dawn of the automobile. For those who might remember, Christopher Reeves and Jane Seymour starred in the movie "Somewhere in Time" where a guy sees the picture of a beautiful woman and tries to move himself back in time. He succeeds and falls in love with Jane Seymour. Unfortunately, he brought some coins with him in his pocket that, if he looked at them, would transport him back to 1980. He accidently did exactly that, and found himself back in his own time. He mourned the loss of his love and lived a miserable existence of depression for the rest of his life. All of it occurred right there on Mackinaw Island at the Grand Hotel.

When you look at how Shakespeare made a satire on the vagaries and stupidities of love with Romeo and Juliet where they kill themselves, the author of "Somewhere in Time" also showed the silliness of love, and its power over humans. Kings have given up their thrones for women and men sacrificed fortunes chasing after beautiful maidens. If you look at America's 'royals', also known as actors, you see the Brad Pitt-Angelina Jolie fairytale turned sour along with hundreds of others in that vacuous magazine: People! Ah, love, it makes the world go around, and it also causes a lot of misery, frustration and mental instability. But when you get it right; the world feels full of joy and hope.

We took a boat to the Lower Peninsula of Michigan. We picked up Route 23 south along the coast line of Lake Huron. We reached Rogers City for a fabulous dinner, and low and behold, Gerry and Don talked me into another motel. I told them, "This is the most motels I have slept in ever in my touring life. I'm turning into a wuss."

"A comfortable one at that," Don Said. "Tell me you don't like a shower and warm floor with your mattress."

"Yeah, you're so comforting," I said.

As I stood there in the shower, I noticed that hot water, a good meal and comfortable motel room wasn't half bad. Oh, no, I must be falling in love with comfort.

(Don watching his shadow grow to 100 feet as it danced across the
highway into the fields beyond. This was a magical 10 miles of later
afternoon touring when everything flowed to the beat of the universe.)

CHAPTER 22

Bicycle travel, dance of imagination on two wheels

"You got to be crazy to ride your bicycle across the country," a man at a convenience store said as we parked the bikes for a rest break. "You're insane," said a college coed on an overlook of the Big Sur. "Why don't you get a horse or something that will carry you?" a cowboy said to me in Montana. "You couldn't get me to ride a bike across America if you put a Smith and Wesson to my head," said one Texan in Amarillo. "I'd be too scared to do something that crazy," an old lady said, on Route 66. FHW

For certain, most people show great trepidation when confronted with something they cannot comprehend. It's out of their life-time scope of experiences. Especially in present day America, comfort, ease and grace take center stage for 90 percent of the population. Why strain yourself in athletic pursuits when you can drive a car, ride a motorcycle, steer a snow machine, ride in a power boat or enjoy a dune buggy?

If a person enjoys a Barker Lounger with a remote more than a bicycle ride, windsurfing, kite boarding, powder ski day or climbing a mountain—so be it. A person may not appreciate any kind of endeavor until he or she experiences it.

What do you consider that "edge" in your spirit that propels you down the road on a bicycle for thousands of miles?

Here's a 10-minute video made by a female world bicycle traveler that might give you an idea of what it's like. To say the least, she's beautiful, tough, determined, classy and lives on the edge of wonder: "Pedal"— https://vimeo.com/237284378

Riding in the Lower Peninsula of Michigan gives a similar feel for the land, but a change in the people. Yes, all of them prove kind, friendly and hardworking. However, the "Uppers" show a wilder streak of independence because they live in northern climes, and they seem somewhat detached from Lower Michigan.

We rode all morning along Lake Huron on Route 23. We passed many harbors and lakes. Often, we kicked-up cranes and egrets from streams or ponds along the road. The woods dominated the landscape. We passed Grand Lake with many summer homes along the seashore. Back and forth, we watched Lake Huron as a vast ocean. Huge, blue, waters sparkled all the way to the horizon.

After 75 miles, we stopped in a Norman Rockwell city, Harrisville, with 150-year-old buildings. A 65-year-old lady pedaled up to us and engaged us in conversation. She looked incredibly fit, but upon dismounting from her bike, she limped badly on her leg. Seems her femur broke while running with her dog at a competition show. She allowed the surgeon to insert a plastic brace into the femur, but it broke, too. She endured another operation with 18 months of rehab. Unfortunately, it clearly didn't allow her to walk with ease.

She raced in Ironman Triathlons and competed in criterion races along with kayaking for 45 years. Nancy exhibited enormous energy, but the past 24 months proved miserable and it messed with her head. Yet she spoke excitedly about being able to bike 12 miles that day.

She offered us her shower, carpeted floor and dinner. We accepted her kindness and followed her down to her lake house. Her garage featured kayaks, bicycles, skis and all sorts of sports gear.

While talking, we discovered that we both graduated from MSU. She loved travel and totally loved life. Instead of being depressed, she anticipated the future.

Off the next morning, we rode from Harrisville to Bay City. We pedaled over flat-as-a-pancake landscape with ample views of Lake Huron. Three Great Lakes down and two to go. The route featured motels and summer cottages for hundreds of Michiganders.

At one point, I stopped at a drug store to buy new shoe laces. A lady talked to me about how inspired she felt by our travels on bicycles. At that point, I fell behind Don and Gerry. About three miles out of town, southbound, a man drove in front of me, parked and waved me to stop. He held a bag of chocolates and two cold water bottles.

"Hi, my name is Tim," he said. "I saw your sign about riding across the USA and wanted to welcome you to Standish. I raced back to my shop to get some chocolates, but you were gone. I then raced up Route 55, but you weren't there. So, I gunned it down 23 to catch you, and so I did. I marvel at your journey. I wish I could take a ride, but I'm too old at 70."

"Tim, thank you," I said. "But you're never too old. I'm 70, too!"

"What?" Tim gasped. "You're 70 years old? You're truly an inspiration."

"Thank you."

He bantered about his chocolatier shop and the best chocolates in those parts. He wanted to gift me on my journey.

"Take care and be safe," he said, as he jumped into his car and drove off.

At the end of the summer, I sent him a packet of my "Spirit of Adventure" greeting cards to thank him. I bet the gift surprised him like few others. I did the same gifting with Nancy. It's a nice gesture to thank people with a special gift for their kindness along the way.

Tim showed me a few things: that humans love to give a part of themselves and cyclists inspire them with their journeys. This thing called "bicycle travel" excites others' spirits. It enthralls others' needs to leave the common, day-to-day existence and to dare to wander, dare to explore, dare to challenge themselves. Long distance bicycle travel becomes a dance of imagination on two wheels. It's a song no balladeer can sing unless moved by the music of rotating spokes and the constant motion of the pedals turning 360 degrees in their own quest to take their rider to amazing moments and sights around the world.

What drives us to glide onto that bicycle dance floor of life? For starters, it's a combination of 'true grit' and free energy applied to a steel frame connected to two spoked wheels wrapped in rubber clouds of wanderlust. If you possess it, you ride into it; if you don't, you won't. For those who possess it, the distant horizon calls you to adventure.

That night, around the campfire, Gerry asked for another epic moment in my world travels. I told a story about taking a turn onto a dirt road with unexpected results:

> "Two roads diverged in a wood, and I…
> I took the one less traveled by,
> and that has made all the difference."
> Robert Frost

Doug, a cycling friend I met in New Zealand, and I decided to ride a border-to-border USA trip in April to follow the spring flowers and view the bird migration patterns. We started in Mexicali, Mexico on our way to Canada through California, Oregon and Washington. We rode through logging country in northern California.

Four weeks into the ride, we woke up beside placid waters with a gray mist hanging low over the mountains in northern California. Slender wisps of moisture played upon the mirror images of trees, while Canada geese, grebes and mallards trumpeted their morning songs.

After breaking camp, we pedaled along a logging highway. Monstrous trucks rumbled past us. Their first draft blew us off the road and seconds later, threatened to suck us back into their rear duel wheels. It didn't make for peaceful riding. A glance at the map gave us an alternative.

We turned up a dirt road heading in a northerly direction. It got rougher on a route less traveled. Because of the corrugated gravel, our hands took a pounding for hours. Nonetheless, it was worth getting away from the trucks. Our chances of seeing wildlife grew tenfold. Going into the wilderness was like looking at the surface of the ocean—nothing on top, but just below the water, a parade of creatures swims in those depths. The woods, too, has an array of creatures living in its branches, on the forest floor, over the meadows and in the lakes.

Another surprise along a dirt road—peacefulness. Not quiet like silence, but a quiet away from machinery—where the wind purrs through the trees on its unhurried journey up a mountain side. I hear birds chirping, squawking, arguing and flapping their wings everywhere in the forest. A woodpecker rat-a-tat-tats against a dead tree trunk while chickadees fly loop-d-loops in the meadow. Insects, too, inhabit the woods; butterflies flutter from wildflower to wildflower. Crickets chirp a symphony of sound whenever I pass by a bog. Bullfrogs add their low notes. The admission to this grand performance stems from the simple price of my pedaling efforts.

The colors keep me enthralled. Pine green proves pointy and leaf green fades to soft. Cattail green goes long and white moss green turns spongy. Yellow flowers dot the green along with white, purple and orange petals chiming in for contrast. Tree bark colors add their own special flavor.

This dirt road stretched more than fifty miles in the middle of northern California snaking its way toward Mount Shasta. Not far along the dirt, we stopped by a lake with a dozen islands in the middle, loaded with birds and ducks. It provided a sanctuary for raising families. A variety of calls echoed across the water.

We rode up to a clearing where four antelope bounded across the road, saw us, then hastily ran back into the woods, their white patched butts bouncing like pogo sticks until they vanished. Off to the side, a muskrat paddled its way across a pond where several ducks fed on grubs.

The woods grew thick, sometimes thin, and rose or fell depending on the terrain. A group of mule deer hopped across a ridge. The road led down into a valley with Mount Shasta on the horizon and a pink sunset coloring long white clouds outlining the sky.

Our campfire flickered beneath a stand of pine trees that seemed to be in the midst of a whole mountainside of lava rocks. It was as if the rocks had exploded from somewhere up the mountain. We rode our bikes in the region near the Ring of Fire, where volcanic mountains dominate the Cascade Range. As we sat there, a pack of coyotes howled at a crescent moon.

In the morning, the sun rose through the mist lighting up 14,179-foot Mount Shasta that dwarfed four other peaks around it. We soon enjoyed a clear sky and view of the snow-covered cone of the dormant volcano.

With a nip in the air, we began our continued slow descent on a two percent grade through thinning trees as we dropped to 3,300 feet. A wide valley stretched before us. We continued on hard packed dirt. A half dozen gray squirrels darted across the road, and we heard birds chirping in the woods.

Out of the trees, we rolled through farmland. Off to our right, a flat field of short grass had not been cultivated for more than a year. Above the field, a red-tailed hawk fluttered in midair. Suddenly, it dropped like a dagger and skimmed three feet off the ground at high speed.

"It's looking for food," Doug said.

"Yeah, but they usually look for it way up high."

"That's right," he said. "That bird is too close to the ground to do anything even if it saw something. It would be going too fast to stop."

Five seconds later, the hawk back-flapped its wings and in a cloud of dust, crashed into the ground much like a shortstop diving for a line drive, and when it caught a rodent, it rolled over with the prize clutched in its talons facing the sky. Abruptly, flapping its wings, the bird righted itself. No fight, no death struggle, no sound. Seconds later, the hawk lifted into the sky with a field mouse in its talons.

"My God, that was incredible!" Doug said.

"Did you see how fast she stopped?" I added.

"On a dime with a nickel's change," he said.

"What a way to start a morning ride," I said.

As if nature was trying to show off its best efforts, another show was in the making. We pedaled past a pond near the highway. Because of our silence, animals become startled after we're already on top of them. At the pond's edge, six Canada geese suddenly sprinted across the water, wings flapping wildly, trying to break free of the surface. We saw their foot marks in the water as they ran across the pond. Within seconds, their black and white colors exploded out of the water with a flurry of wings climbing into the sky. Once airborne, they flew into Mount Shasta's snowfields.

"Who are we supposed to pay for this morning's show?" Doug asked.

"Maybe we'll have to pull a ten-mile, 14 percent uphill grade," I said.

Another five minutes along the way, we crested a ridge. Three volcanic peaks thrust into the sky before us. Mount Lassen, Cinder Cone, and Shasta poked through cloudbanks. Maybe California didn't want us to leave. It had already shown us Yosemite, the Yuba Valley, the 49er trail, and now this.

Fifteen minutes down the road, five mule deer ran up a ridge on our right, and out of sight.

"Bet those guys are long gone," I said.

"They weren't waiting around for us...hey look!" Doug yelled.

Five deer crossed the road, not twenty yards in front of us. They jumped over a fence. They leaped like a jack-in-the-box on four legs at once. One by one, they glided over the fence and vanished behind the hill.

"I can't take this kind of nature overload so early in the morning," I said. "It can't get any better than this."

We cranked along until we crossed through the middle of a marsh. Again, nature jumped up in the form of wings everywhere. Canada honkers poked their heads out from tall grasses, while mallards rushed into flight when we startled them. Grebes hugged their hiding places in the deep grass. Black birds, sparrows, and birds of every color and description lived in the marsh. Each possessed a different song and flew with a variety of wing beats.

"You know," Doug said. "We're so lucky to see these wild wings on parade."

"You got that right," I said.

At the Route 299 intersection, we met a toy maker and his wife. While we talked, more than five hundred head of cattle bolted up the road behind us. A few cowboys on horseback drove the herd toward pastureland higher up the valley. We didn't think much about it as they passed, but that was the direction we were headed. Five minutes later, we said goodbye to the toy maker and began climbing out of the valley.

Have you ever followed a herd of 500 cows on a bicycle? Neither had we, until that morning. At first it was funny seeing how the males peed as they walked, leaving watery "S" trails in the road. When the females peed, they stopped and made a large splash. The big problem was how they performed their morning constitutional. They filled the road with land mines in the form of cow pies. It got so thick at times, we couldn't avoid it. At first, we navigated around the splash piles by steering in circle eights. Except the more we pedaled, the thicker the minefield became, until cow poop squeezed up from our tires into our brake pads. At one tight juncture in the road, I turned hard to miss one cow pie. It was one of those pies where the cow took the time to stand in one place and build up a large green mound. I swerved to avoid it, but my front tire, already mired in green goosh, lost traction. Down I went, left hand outstretched, headed for the steaming green cow pie. Splat! My hand made a perfect five fingered landing right into the middle of a rather warm, squishy, pile of poop. My bike and panniers fell into two other piles near the one where my hand was now implanted.

"Nothing like getting close to the good green earth," Doug said, as he pulled up next to me. "You always were one to get your hands into everything."

"That's not funny," I said, pulling my hand from the cow pie.

We laughed. I grabbed my paper towel roll out of my day pack and began wiping the stuff from between my fingers, off my arm and off the panniers. Next, I squirted my water bottles over my hand to clean the remaining poop away.

We mounted the bikes and rode through the remaining mile of "natural obstacles." Soon, we cranked up a 1,500-foot grade out of the valley. As we neared the top, the view from where we had come to where we stood was filled with memories.

Our experiences reminded me of what Henry David Thoreau once wrote: "We need the tonic of the wilderness, to wade sometimes in the marsh where the bitten and meadow hen lurk, and hear the booming of the snipe; to smell the whispering sedge where only some wilder and more solitary fowl builds her nest, and the mink crawls with its belly close to the ground."

We turned up a dirt road today, and it was more than worth it.

(View of the road from the perspective of a cyclist. If you closely, you can see a rainbow up ahead in the "V" of the trees over the road.)

CHAPTER 23

Bicycling as an addictive habit that's incurable

"Long distance bicycle adventure up-levels a person toward lofty heights while pedaling the Rocky Mountains. It drenches a person in the mystical enchantment of the Amazon rainforests. Cycling heats up a cyclist's body while crossing the Australian Outback. But whatever test it provides, bicycle adventure combines the best attributes of humanity: simplicity, passion and purpose. When you see such a person on tour, you witness the glory of the human body, mind and spirit in blissful locomotion." FHW

When you git down the road, the road gits in your craw. It mesmerizes your entire being. You taste certain flavors created by pedaling over the long haul. Many try to describe it, but it's much like sex. If you haven't experienced it, no amount of explanation will bring you up to speed. You're kinda' listening to the stories, but nothing computes.

"What are they talking about and why do they think it's so delicious?" you ask.

As I said, when you git down the road, the road gits in your craw. It grabs you by your spirit, places a subtle grip on your soul, and for the life of me, it hasn't let go. Maybe it's an addiction. But what kind of addiction? Is it good for you or bad for you? Is it like alcohol, heroin or pot?

At one point in my twenties, I visited a psychiatrist for some consultation.

"Dr. Hamilton," I said. "I tried this bicycle touring stuff and it's got me by the throat. I mean, it's got me by the…well, it's hard to explain. I can't seem to pin it down, but each day, it forces me to ride my bike into the unknown. At dawn, I wake up in my tent, and I look forward to riding that damned bike. In fact, I can't stop myself. I'm hooked. I'm addicted. I'm hopelessly out of control and don't know what to do about it."

"What kind of symptoms are you feeling," Dr. Hamilton asked.

"You know," I said. "I get sweaty palms. Sweaty brow. Sweat beads up on my arms and little sweat droplets drain down the back of my spine. Sometimes my quads burn. At other times, I can't stop pedaling up mountains or on the flats. I'm hooked beyond explanation. Worse case, sweat drips off my nose and many times, into my eyes, stinging them."

"Sounds like a bad case," Dr. Hamilton said.

"So, do you have something I can take to break this addiction?" I asked. "Either I break this addiction or it's going to carry me on some kind of fantasy ride around the world with no understanding of where I might end up. Will I live or will I die? Will I have any friends to help me recover? There's a lot of unknowns that really frighten me. I'm too young to die."

"Son," he said. "Here's my best prescription…I want you to get on that bike any time you feel the addiction taking over your body. Ride like the wind. Ride into the thick of life. If you feel miserable in a rain storm, gnash your teeth and ride through it. If you find yourself being bashed by headwinds, dare them to stop you, in fact, plow through them like a Coast Guard Cutter. Become a man possessed.

"If you're climbing a 12,000-foot mountain pass, just let the addiction take over your body to get you to the top. Be sure to laugh at the mountain gods as you enjoy the alpine beauty all around you. Sometimes addictions cannot be cured. It's possible that you are hopelessly addicted to such an extent that death is the only solution. If you don't choose death, you must soldier onward."

The doctor continued, "On a desert plain, boring as hell, hot as hades, kinda' like the Outback or the Atacama Desert, just command your legs to tough it out. And finally, if you take my advice, I say to keep riding your bicycle. **It will put you on the road to recovery for as long as it takes.**"

"Okay doc," I said. "From what you're telling me, I guess there's no cure."

"You got that right, Frosty," said Dr. Hamilton. "I'm sorry that I can't be of much help."

"That's okay doc," I said. "You said, 'ride into the thick of life...' yup, I can do that."

Rain threatened as we rode into the north side of Bay City, Michigan after a long day. We pulled into an abandoned church yard off Route 23. No one around, but grave sites. It's very quiet camping in a graveyard. There's no one alive to bother you for a good night's sleep. Of course, if you read any of Stephen King, you might attract nightmares. Me? I snore all night long with no one complaining. I slept like a baby in a bassinette.

We cranked into Bay City for breakfast at a Big Boy Restaurant; very famous in Michigan. Cutting across the thumb on Route 16 to Route 46, we rode along flatter-than-a-pancake farm land with fruit stands, endless farms and tiny villages. Not wanting to miss fresh fruit, we bought apples, black berries and peaches. We ended up in Sandusky where we enjoyed an impromptu lunch with firefighting crews. They guided us over to a huge gazebo in the town park and showers in the gym.

"Not a bad place to camp," Don said. "It looks like rain."

"Yup, lots of rain in the forecast the fireman said," Gerry added.

That night, rain fell unceasingly, and when we awoke, more rain fell around us.

For the next four hours, we rode in a constant downpour. We switched on our red and white LED blinking lights. We splashed through a thick layer of water on the pavement. Green grass exploded in the fields and yellow flowers glistened along the road. Above us, a gray, rainy sky sliced downward in a constant curtain of water.

"This sucks," Don said.

"It more than sucks," Gerry added. "We need a new tour director. Tell me why we're following Frosty, again? What does he have against us?"

"Okay, you guys," I said. "Go home to your mothers if you can't tolerate a little liquid sunshine."

After five hours of flying down the road like three soaked ducks, feathers drooping, frowns on our faces and deflated, water-drenched feelings of liquid misery—the sky broke open with blue stretching eastward to the horizon.

"A-friggin' men," said Don.

"Let's stop at that sub shop to dry off," I said.

An hour later, we jumped on a 25 mile per hour tailwind all the way to Port Sanilac. We ate lunch in another one of those restaurants with walls filled with fur, feathers and fins. We headed south on Route 25 all the way to Port Huron where a bridge carried us over to Canada. After clearing customs, we visited the visitor center before making our way eastward toward Niagara Fall on Route 402. Pretty much a straight shot to the falls.

At that point in the ride, we all lost a few pounds. Our legs felt like coiled bands of steel. We featured toned arms and piston-like thighs able to hammer out 100 miles without thinking about it. We slept like rocks at night and ate like Kansas combines devouring everything in our paths. If you asked Gerry, he might pull out his guitar, "Life is good on a bicycle. It's the only way to see the USA and beyond."

(Many signs along adventure highway surprise and delight cyclists.
Many clever signs brought a great deal of laughter to our days.)

CHAPTER 24

Canada, A Beautiful Country

"A new country, a new culture, a new language, a new opportunity for enthralling experiences on this planet. Each cyclist crosses world boundaries to discover the varieties of humanity on an intimate level at 12 miles per hour. We don't fly in, pay for a bus trip around the city, eat at elegant restaurants, and sleep in fancy motels. We don't wear pressed pants and fancy shirts. Women cyclists lack makeup and the frilly dresses and high heels that boast a cosmopolitan slant. We don't carry an 'air' of attitude, wealth or privilege. When long-distance touring cyclists reach across a new country's boundary, he or she becomes an ambassador of peace, friendship and inspiration. One of the great gifts of bicycle travel manifests in each cyclist's extraordinary ability to bring his or her understandings, patience and humility to each new country visited. In many ways, a cyclist becomes the finest ambassador for his or her country, because the citizens of countries around the world enjoy the bare-bones freedom

as well as commonality of humanity within cyclists and within each of us." FHW

We jumped on Route 6 to Route 39 to Straitray. We pedaled along farm fields loaded with corn, wheat, hat, soybeans, strawberry patches and clothes hanging on lines in farmers' yards.

The road shot straight across Ontario, Canada. We saw Lake Erie on our right. Within two days, we neared Niagara Falls from the Canadian side. As we pedaled through one small village, the cable to my rear derailleur broke. It left me with one high gear and three front chain rings. As I looked for my spare cable in my panniers, I discovered that I had not replaced the spare cable from a previous break. I needed to find a bike shop.

"Looks like I've got to wait until Niagara Falls to buy a shift cable," I said.

"No big deal," said Don.

As we rode into Niagara Falls, I asked a mechanic at an oil change shop for directions to a bike store. He said, "Over the next hill and take the first left. His name is Colin. He'll take care of you."

Ten minutes later, we walked into a fully loaded bike shop and hockey gear sales. Colin replaced the cable and tuned my rear derailleur system in 45 minutes.

"What's the damage?" I asked.

"You're all set. No charge. Pay it forward," he said.

He wouldn't take a dime. No amount of urging him with my cash or credit card would sway him.

"You're so kind Colin," I said. "Expect a little something in the mail in four weeks when I finish this ride."

One of the things Colin showed during my short stay warmed my heart. He sharpened the edges of skates for several boys while the parents waited. After giving them their skates, he hugged them with powerful words of praise and encouragement to get out there and play their best hockey. As a former teacher, he touched me deeply. We need men and women to give kids a strong sense of themselves. We need to encourage their way in the world. Colin proved a fine man and mentor.

Of course, when I returned home, I sent him a copy of my book: **Living Your Spectacular Life**, and 10 "Spirit of Adventure" greeting cards. I suspect he enjoyed the surprise. And, of course, I pass forward his kindness every chance I get.

We rolled through city traffic until we reached the highly glitzy, overly commercialized city near the falls. Every kind of tourist trap surrounded the falls with Ripley's Believe it or Not, to the House of Dungeons and Dragons. People from all over the world with costumes from dozens of countries, brought colors of the rainbow to the scene.

We rode over to the falls. What happened next blew our minds.

We saw the water raging over the precipice of the falls. At the same time, the mist created an enormous rainbow across the chasm. Then, people started yelling about the eclipse of the sun and pointing. We grabbed dark glasses from a vendor to see a quarter of the sun blackened by the moon.

"Good grief," I said. "This is a mind-bending trifecta of natural phenomena occurring right at this moment as we hit Niagara Falls."

"Sure is beautiful," said Gerry.

"Never in my wildest dreams did I think I would ride my bicycle across North America to see such sights," said Don. "Can I count this as one of those 'moments' you talked about?"

"You got it, man," I said, smiling. "I keep my promises that you will ride into those unique moments that will last forever in your memories."

Quickly, the eclipse faded to reveal the entire sun shining down upon us. The rainbow continued arching over the Niagara chasm. The "Maid of the Mist" tourist boat plowed into the roaring white water of the falls below us. Hundreds of people snapped pictures of themselves and the falls. Green grass, cut to perfection, led to dozens of flower beds along the walkways.

And still, people discarded their trash on the grass and sidewalk—even with trash cans placed every 30 yards along the walk. To see so much beauty, but to see people trashing it as they look at so much beauty—mystifies me to no end. Ironically, I saw two litter picker-uppers hauling around their trash bags with sticks to pick up bottles and trash with a small clamp at the end of the metal stick.

It makes for a metaphor of how humanity treats this planet wondrous planet: very poorly as to trashing the biosphere with chemicals, spoiling the oceans with plastics, and degrading the land with human garbage on a scale heretofore unknown in the history of human race. I'm sure Mother Nature weeps at the onslaught and the animals cringe when humans invade their natural world.

After five fabulous hours talking with other tourists, we took tons of flower pictures, ate more food, and finally, rode the bikes across the bridge into New York State.

After inquiring around, the $300.00 per room motel rates pretty much rendered us financially exhausted thinking about it. We rode out of town until we found a mowed field of grass along the highway behind a bunch of trees. A big tractor blocked the entrance from the road to give us a nice, private camp spot just out of the city.

For certain, that day, we experienced a monumental 'moment' in the 'trifecta' we witnessed with the falls, rainbow and eclipse of the sun. It's happened many times on my rides around the planet. Only one other falls that I've seen in my world travels exceeds Niagara, and that's Falls de Iguassu on the corner of Brazil, Paraguay and Uruguay. It's bigger and thicker water cascading over the rocks. It stands out in the middle of a jungle with toucan birds, brilliant butterflies, jungle flowers galore, and wild animals everywhere. Unfortunately, it's so remote that most people cannot visit it.

Because of such moments in my world travels, I created a memory shelf 40 years ago to hold all the mementos that I collected in my journeys across six continents. It's a big long cabinet with four shelves. I filled each shelf with melted snow from Antarctica and rocks from that frozen continent. It includes fans from Japan, bolo lariats from Argentina, a boomerang from Australia, cow bells from Switzerland, rocks from Norway, five sets of small water bottles from two oceans from my coast-to-coast rides, jade from China, brass vases from India, bamboo walking stick from Nepal, carvings from Mexico, shells from the Galapagos Island, teeth from grizzly bears in Alaska, pine needles from redwoods, and dozens of other artifacts from around the world. Each morning, I walk through the living room to see the array of my memories. It brings a smile to my face to know that I chased my dreams, caught my dreams and lived my dreams. I am forever thankful for the friends and people who supported my travels all these years of my life's journey.

(Frosty standing on the rim of Canada's side of Niagara Falls. He witnessed
a trifecta of natural wonders with the falls, a rainbow and the eclipse of
the sun, all in five minutes. This trifecta caused one of those "edge of
wonder" moments that occur while riding your bike across a continent.)

CHAPTER 25

History Revealed from the American Revolution

"As the days run into nights on a cross continent bicycle adventure, your body transforms into a sinewy, powerhouse of blood, guts and muscle. Your mind tackles mountain grades with eager tenacity. Your body responds with obstinate enthusiasm. You experience the power of your internal being on a level seldom tapped by average human beings. You transform your days from average to spectacular. You live on the edge of wonder mentally, physically and spiritually. You devour food, you suck great amounts of air into your heaving lungs, which in turn, power your legs that spin the wheels toward epic moments. Flats? Mountains? Rain? Heat? Sweat? Bring it on! Bicycling lets you know you're outrageously alive. Why do you raise your hands in triumph at breathtaking moments? Because you cannot help but let the universe know you live a spectacular life!" FHW

Sometimes, you must take a break. After pounding the pedals for 10 days or longer, a rest day gives your body a chance to relax. It gives your muscles a moment to renew.

Also, you enjoy a chance to reflect, write, review your life goals, your adventure goals, your relationships with friends and yourself.

After that day of rest, your mind, spirit and legs once again feel like a new-born colt, ready to spring into action.

We rode hard into the woods of New York State. After twenty miles, we watched a menacing black cloud creep in from the east.

"We're about to be pissed on by the storm gods," Don said.

"Let's find a place to hang out," Gerry said.

Sure enough, 10 minutes later, we reached a motel in a small town. After registering, we pushed the bikes into the room. The sky opened up. I mean, it drove rain down into the tiling on the roof and smashed against the pavement. It slammed against the windows with the fury of a thousand devils.

"Glad to be out of that unkind weather," Gerry said.

We showered, shaved and washed clothes. We sat around reading and writing for the rest of the day. The rains poured out of that New York sky. No mercy, no care, unrelenting, punishing—but we could care less. We enjoyed a roof over our heads.

Next morning, blue skies! Yahoo!

We rolled along the lake. We stopped at some shops by the lake when one lady gave me a pen light from a 400 mile walk she took to fund cancer research. Another lady lamented the loss of her county to an invasion of people. "Too crowded," she said. "And getting worse every summer."

We rolled along Lake Ontario all day with flat land, trees, blue lake, endless birds, flowers and sunshine. Yes, it's good to be alive!

Route 18 carried us through much beauty. Easy pedaling! Easy living! Lots of fruit stands. Lots of wine tasting outlets. We stopped in Hilton, New York to ask some kids where to camp.

"At the carnival grounds about a quarter mile down 18," they said.

We pedaled between two buildings for perfect privacy with toilets and showers at our command.

It's too cool to have no idea where you're going to camp, yet, something always turns up. Creative stealth camping. I could write a book about the interesting places I have set down my tent stakes. Each place proves unique beyond comparison.

We cruised through Rochester at 3,750 miles thus far on Route 104 to Route 404. Only 550 more miles to Bar Harbor.

"Gees," I said. "We're running out of continent. We'll reach the Atlantic within a week."

"Not sure I want this ride to end," said Don.

"Me, neither," said Gerry.

"Know the feeling, dudes," I said.

Again, more corn, wheat and hay fields, plus apple orchards along with pumpkins galore.

"Ah, God created cantaloupe melons for cyclists," Gerry said.

We stopped in Walcott to camp in a field behind the mall. We endured trash and crap all over the place.

In the morning, we headed into the Adirondack Mountains in Upstate New York. During that section of the ride, my brain dwelled on my father and mother, both deceased. When mom died two years ago, the anchor vanished. Then, thinking about my father, and not being able to let him know what kind of a man he created in me—just made me melancholy. But over the years, I learned to accept it because there's nothing to do about it. Fate deals you a hand and you play it. Thankfully, my parents gave me a good hand and the ability to play the game of life in a positive and fruitful way.

We awakened in the morning to pack and eat a fine breakfast at a local Tim Horten's Restaurant. They served really great oatmeal with blackberries.

At lunch, we stopped in a small town with a down-home restaurant. I saw a picture of a teen, sitting on a bench with a hockey stick in his hand. He died from a drunk driver.

I talked to the waitress about it, "He was my son."

"Ohhh," I said. "I'm so sorry."

"It's the way it is," she said. "I miss him every day."

We dried the tents out in the sunshine before taking off. We took photographs of a Venus de Milo statue in the center of the town. The city fathers placed the statue there in 1834 where it stands today.

We jumped on Route 370 that carried us past lots of woods, corn fields and farm houses. All of them out of the 1800's. Some looked like Thomas Jefferson's Monticello with Greek columns adorning the fronts. Pretty impressive. Where money abounds at any age, rich people create outsized homes. Those homes matched their egos and bank accounts.

We pedaled onto Route 31 at Baldwinsville and continued through the deep woods. We stopped in Cato, New York at the Cato Hotel that resembled the same architecture as George Washington's home in Mt. Vernon outside of Washington DC. The huge columns in front gave it away at 250 years old. Inside, the wood smelled old. The bar reeked of age and the glass reflected dozens of generations of beer and whiskey drinkers. At first, they came in coonskin caps and horses, to be followed by buggies and then, stage coaches. Travelers, trappers and statesmen! History surrounded us.

We stopped in Bridgeport, New York. We pedaled Route 31 to a bicycle shop. We pedaled around the back to find a patch of green for camping. Also, an outhouse.

"Gees Louise," Don said. "This is perfect."

Up early, we stopped at Kay's & Tony's for breakfast. Everyone stepping into the restaurant approached us about my sign on the back of my bike: Pacific to Atlantic. They loved it.

They asked the usual questions: "How many miles do you travel a day?" "Why are you doing this?" "How does it feel to be as old as dirt and still ride a bicycle?" "What are you trying to prove?" "You guys inspired my wife and me."

As we sat there, Don broke out a map of the USA. He marked the entire route. The red line from his pen grew long and the blank spaces still awaiting us grew short. I teared up for a moment.

One couple wanted to hear our story. We gave them quite a good rendition of our adventures across North America.

We rolled along on Route 31 that passed by the southern side of a very long lake. More fruit stands. We devoured apples, pears, peaches, strawberries and blue berries.

Finally, we reached Rome, New York with its Fort Still. We used it to conquer the Native Americans. Forts created territorial markers and whites plotted their quests with forts and roads. Each town presented a sign showing when it began. Most towns began in the 1700's. Elegant homes with old architecture dotted the road.

Pedaling on Route 365, we headed into Adirondack Park. New Yorkers preserved it for its divine beauty. We pedaled into Trenton, New York. A man invited us to stop in back of his hotel to camp in a nice green spot. He told us of Trenton's history. Good grief! George Washington fought in that area.

More amazing, President Grant stepped out on the veranda of second floor of the Trenton Hotel to give a speech. We stood in the same exact spot where he gave the speech. Also, President Woodrow Wilson visited the hotel where he carried on a tryst with his lover for several years. He wouldn't get away with it in this day and age.

"People are always shouting they want to create a better future. It's not true. The future is an apathetic void of no interest to anyone. The past is full of life, eager to irritate us, provoke and insult us, tempt us to destroy or repaint it. The only reason people want to be masters of the future is to change the past." – **Milan Kundera**

(As you can see, bicycle riders like to raise their hands at a moment of triumph. It's almost like celebrating your joy with the universe. That's Frosty reaching New York State.)

CHAPTER 26

The Portals of Old Age

"History is always written by the winners. When two cultures clash, the loser is obliterated, and the winner writes the history books—books which glorify their own cause and disparage the conquered foe. As Napoleon once said, 'What is history, but a fable agreed upon?'" — Dan Brown, The Da Vinci Code

Riding through upstate New York throws a cyclist into the guts of America's Revolutionary War. It also throws a rider into the manifest destiny of Europeans as they conquered the Native Americans across North America. History tells us that 522 tribes lived in territorial sectors from Mexico to Alaska.

When the white man brought diseases, approximately 90 percent of Native Americans died from small pox, measles, mumps, flu and other viruses. Such diseases and warfare doomed most of the tribes.

While forgotten in the history books by the conquering Europeans, those aboriginal people lived, worked and thrived in the forest, deserts, mountains and seashores of America. Today, they languish on reservations or what I call "internment camps" created by the

Europeans. Dan Brown's quote sums it up. Several other books also describe it: **Sand Creek Massacre, Bury My Heart at Wounded Knee** and **Trail of Tears.** It's rough reading for anyone with a heart.

At the same time, no civilization remains permanent. From the march of history, even the United States faces a tenuous future. While we're witnessing it first hand as glorious victories for the settlers, somebody else lost their freedoms, ways of life, religion and cultures. In many ways, the history of humanity remains a bloody, brutal and merciless march into the future.

We pedaled out of Trenton, New York under sunny skies. The road wound its way through the deep forests like a giant anaconda snake. Lakes and rivers cut through the woods.

Now into September, the first colors of autumn touched some underbrush and maple trees—bronze, gold, topaz, crimson, lavender, yellow and magenta.

We climbed a long hill to a huge reservoir lake. We stopped to take pictures when a family drove up.

"You guys are close to the Atlantic," the father said. "What a remarkable adventure for you boys."

"Thank you," said Don.

We regaled the family with our best stories of the trip. Their kids hung on every word. They looked at us as brave explorers with epic conquests from our bicycle travels. They loved the stories of our journey along the Lewis & Clark Trail.

For the rest of the day, we endured grinding up hills and coasting down the other side. Late in the day, I fell behind Gerry and Don. As I approached a downhill with guard rail. My rear tire blew out.

"Dang," I said. "Why a rear tire?"

Forty minutes later, after finishing the repair, I piled all my gear on the bike when a car stopped. A kid walked over with a pizza box and two bottles of cold water.

"My dad saw you fixing your flat tire when we passed you 45 minutes ago," he said. "He wanted you to have this pizza and drinks."

I looked over at the father, "Thank you, sir!" He gave me a thumbs up. The kid walked back over to the car and jumped into the back seat. They drove off.

That pizza tasted so good. People prove themselves beautiful. You can bet that events like that make me look forward to paying kindness forward.

Kindness must occur in waves. I pedaled to catch up to Gerry and Don when a couple in red convertible passed me waving and yelling. They stopped at the top of the next hill. When I reached them, the woman shook my hand with a drink and $50.00 bill.

"You have inspired us to ride our bikes across Europe next summer," she said. "We've heard so much about bicycle travel from our friends. Your sign clicked for us. We're going to do it, too."

They told their stories while I listened. Their gift blew me into the weeds. People astound me.

Of course, I pass those financial gifts forward when I see a poor person with a sign on a street corner. I pop $10 into his or her hand with a smile and I wish them good health and high spirits.

Finally, at the end of the day, Gerry, Don and I camped at the Bethel Church yard in Lake Pleasant. We enjoyed a rollicking round of storytelling as to gifts, food and money. Even while they rode together, they met a bunch of folks who yearned to ride bikes across the country, too. It seems we inspired a lot of people.

We pedaled into the town of Lake Pleasant on Route 365. We met Rich Lytle, 54, retired, riding his bicycle around the world for the next three years. Married and divorced twice, he just got tired of it all. One daughter was grown and married. He felt time running out to be healthy enough to make such a grand world journey. We enjoyed a great conversational breakfast at a local diner.

We all pedaled down the road toward Lake George. Along the way, a fellow named Nate stopped his car in front of us.

"You're Frosty aren't you," he said, extending his hand.

"How in the hell do you know my name?" I said, shaking hands with him.

"My wife and I met you in Yellowstone on our ride across the USA in 2013," he said. "I never forgot your flags, so I knew it must be you." "I'll be darned," I said.

We bantered for 10 minutes before he had to get going to get to work on time.

"How do you figure that one?" I said to Don.

"Your flags do stick out," Don said.

We reached Route 8 and then Route 9 south to Route 22 south to Lake George. At Route 22, Rich headed north, and we headed south. I still see his posts on Facebook. He's in Bolivia, South America at the latest post.

At a diner in Lake George, we met a 70-year-old canoe racer named Mort Johnson.

"You guys are doing a great thing," he said.

He knew Verlen Kruger, the legendary canoeist who took a 28,000-mile canoe challenge around North America 40 years ago. He then paddled from the Arctic Ocean through all of North America and down the Mississippi River to spit out into the Gulf of Mexico. From there, he paddled across the Gulf to South America and paddled the interior with his wife all the way to the bottom of South America. I actually rode my bicycle the length of South America in 1987-88, and beat him to the bottom in Ushuaia by two weeks. I shared dinner with him and his son in Grand Rapids, Michigan years ago. We're talking mega-adventurers!

Jack expressed his surprise that I personally knew Verlen. Jack complained that, at 70, he suffered all sorts of pain. He endured an enlarged prostate and had to pee every 30 minutes. It made him cranky. He suffered three fused vertebrae in his back. His arthritic hands pained him when he paddled.

"Not fun being 70," he said.

"Well, I'm 70, so I feel your pain," I said.

"You're 70?" he gasped.

"Almost 71," I said.

"Even more congratulations for making 4,000 miles across America," he said.

"Yeah, well, Don turned 70 on this ride," I said.

"Guess we just keep doin' what we're doin' until we die," Mort said.

"That's the plan," Don said. "I find that if I keep pedaling fast enough, I can stay ahead of old age better."

We camped out in the woods that night. I felt the noose of time tightening around my own life, and I know Don felt different about being 70. It's a portal, yet, if we're healthy, we keep moving down the road of life with positive energy, healthy eating and a sense of purpose.

(This house in upstate New York, looked much like
George Washington's near Washington DC.)

CHAPTER 27

Reaching the Atlantic Ocean

"No matter how long your tour, no matter how many miles, no matter how many campfires and no matter how many amazing moments you experienced—your journey ultimately comes to an end. It might be a coast-to-coast, border-to-border or continent-to-continent, but like Thomas Stevens' first bicycle journey around the world 1884 to 1886—you finally come to the finality of your expedition. I think Captain Jean Luc Picard of the Starship Enterprise said it best, 'Someone once said that time stalks us all our lives. I rather believe that time is a companion that goes with us on a journey. It reminds us to cherish each moment, because it will never come again. What we leave behind is not as important as how we lived.' Which means to me: relish the highs, endure the lows and savor the in-between times. Remember the good, bad and ugly moments. Stand tall that you possessed the courage to explore the world on your iron steed. It provided you with wings to fly. It carried you into yet another adventure while it allowed you to live your dreams." FHW

We're heading into New Hampshire with a quick in and out sort of deal. Small state, beautiful state, wilderness galore! It doesn't get much better than that. I'm vibrating different feelings about the day as we near the end of the ride. I'm enjoying flashbacks of wondrous moments of our ride. The Columbia River Gorge looms large in my memory banks. That wildfire across Montana still burns in my mind and the smell remains in my nostrils.

We started in Ediflin and rode to Moultonborough. We ate at Mickey's Restaurant for a breakfast of oatmeal and pancakes. Route 40 turned into Route 104 in Danbury to Meredith, New Hampshire.

We stopped at a sub shop and a lady said her 62-year-old husband wanted to ride across America, "But I won't let him!"

We rolled the bikes into Maine. Same landscape of wilderness, flowers and beautiful country. We pedaled all day until finding a private cut of grass to an abandoned building near a lake. Perfect spot off the highway and totally secluded.

Next day, along Route 25, we passed hundreds of houses and dozens of small towns right out of a Norman Rockwell painting. We camped west of Portland, Maine.

We rode all day, but decided to stop at a motel before a hellacious rainstorm dropped on our heads. As we pulled into the room, the savage skies opened up.

In the morning, blue skies prevailed as we rolled the bikes north toward Bar Harbor, Maine. We pedaled Route 1 all the way to Route 3 into Bar Harbor.

"There's the Atlantic," I yelled as we rolled around one of a million curves on the ride.

"Beautiful," said Gerry.

"Who woulda' thunk it," said Don.

We pedaled around the town until we found some shoreline. We poked our bike tires into the Atlantic Ocean. We high-fived each other.

"Dudes," I said. "Well done!"

"Back at you," said Gerry. "Hell of a ride, hell of a memory! Thanks boys."

"This is the greatest adventure of my life," said Don. "I can hardly cope with what we just accomplished. I love you guys."

"Back at you," I said.

"Bloody hell, mate," Gerry said. "Let's go find a fine restaurant and a good beer."

"Spoken like a true Irishman," I said.

So ended an amazing journey of our bodies, minds and spirits in the summer of 2017. Not much more to say since I've told this tale to the best of my knowledge. For me, the journey provided a tremendous time of friendship, laughter, a few tears, singing with Gerry playing his guitar, fantastic campfires and tons of delicious foods.

However, there's something sad about the end of an adventure. When your high school kid graduates, you cry. When he or she leaves for college or a new life out in the world, you mourn for your own loss. You've spent 18 years with that precious child. At the end of a tense basketball game, you may win or lose, but it's done, never to be repeated. That night on the 4th of July on this trip, we wanted it to last forever, but it ended.

As we pedaled the last couple of days of the ride, unlike Lewis & Clark, we knew our ending neared. They didn't. Because we knew, it pained us to finish such an outstanding event in our lives. Believe me, it's much more significant when you're over 70 and looking at the back end of your life. Every day, every moment, every event and every adventure impact your sense of time, living and eternity.

For certain, we loved Gerry's magical guitar around the campfire, at a bar, at a picnic table and at the most captivating of times. We laughed, we pedaled, and we shared fellowship with one another. Each of us leaves this journey with pictures, words and memories. We lived the times of our lives. Frosty Wooldridge, Don Lindahl, Gerry Mulroy, Robert Case, Frank Cauthorn, coast-to-coast across America, 4,300 miles from Astoria, Oregon to Bar Harbor, Maine.

For Gerry Mulroy, he became the first and only Irishman to bicycle East to West and West to East across North America. Somebody had to be first, so he's the man. And, a huge thank you to Gerry for his guitar and voice, his humor and humanity. Also, a huge part of Gerry's life on the road, his daughter Rosie who we shared laughter over the phone and pictures along the way. Many blessings to Gerry and Rosie on their continued adventures along their journeys. At the end, Gerry took out his trusty guitar to sing, "If I could save time in a bottle, the first thing that I'd like to do; Is to save every day till eternity passes away, just to spend them with you. If I could make days last forever, if words could make wishes come true, I'd save every day like a treasure and then, again I would spend them with you."

For Don, the honor of turning 70 on one of the greatest adventures of his life. He shared his heart, his passions and his loves. He shared his two kids and their kids. He told jokes that kept us laughing and chuckling down the road. Always a bright spirit, he gave the ride his finest and his heart. Don said, "It was an epic journey that summoned the best this body had to offer. It was a combination of all three...... physical, mental, and spiritual, and the gratification I felt on the last day as we put that front wheel into the Atlantic Ocean was beyond words."

For Frank Cauthorn, an Ironman triathlete, a father, mountaineer, skier, backpacker, fisherman, cyclist and sportsman. We loved his energy, his heart and his cycling moxy. He made every day of the ride a splendid time for all of us. Love to ride with him again! And, he completed his coast-to-coast, too. So, in a meaningful way, we all bicycled from the Pacific Ocean to the Atlantic Ocean on the "Edge of Wonder" the entire journey.

For Robert Case, he enjoyed the best of the best on the Lewis & Clark Trail. He became a long-distance touring rider. He learned a few things and taught all of us a few things. May his journey continue in good health and high spirits. Additionally, he completed his coast-to-coast ride the following year.

Don Lindahl, Gerry Mulroy, Robert Case, Frank Cauthorn and Frosty Wooldridge, coast-to-coast across America, 4,300 miles from Astoria, Oregon to Bar Harbor, Maine.

And that's it from here folks! There's the Atlantic Ocean right in front of us.

The End

(Four-masted schooner docked in Bar Harbor, Maine.)

(Gerry and Don touching the Atlantic Ocean.)

(Frosty standing at the Atlantic Ocean.)

CHAPTER 28

You want to bicycle across America or the planet?

"Are you over 60 or 70? Do you want to sit on your butt for the rest of your life without experiencing something epic you accomplished? What's in a lifespan? What's in retirement? What's it like to get your face into the wind? Old age can either kill you with idleness or it can energize you with curiosity, passion and purpose. Bicycle touring renders all three, big time!" FHW

WHAT IT'S LIKE BEING A LONG-DISTANCE BICYCLE RIDER?

"Why are you riding your bicycle across America, sir?" asked a twenty-something.

"It's a long story, son," I replied.

What is it like being a long-distance touring rider? Is it exciting? Does it make traveling special? What makes me do it? How is it traveling on a bicycle? I am asked these questions often while I'm on tour and I try to explain it to folks, but they don't possess the background to understand. Still, I try to explain my feelings.

On an emotional level, it's a sensory involvement with natural forces surrounding me. It's a tasting of the wind, a feeling of the coolness, and the warmth—swirling clouds above me and grasses bending in soft breezes. Touring puts me into intimate contact with sunrises and sunsets.

Along seacoasts, I watch waves charge their white fury against sandy beaches. Touring, in its elegant silence, allows me to see an eagle swoop out of the blue, and with its talons extended, grab a mouse and lift into the sky headed toward its nest. Touring allows me to see a kangaroo hop across the road in Australia or ride into the teeth of an approaching storm.

I witness quiet and wild moments depending on nature. When I am a long-distance touring rider, I get caught up in the forces that swirl around me, and I feel at peace with them. The normal everyday occurrences of life, which seem extraordinary to many people, are normal to me. Why? Because I place myself in a wilderness 'orbit' that synchronizes with the natural, the animal world—far away from the maddening din of humanity's cities.

One of the things I enjoy as I ride along, is the ease with which I move through the natural world. My journey carries me through deserts, mountains, forests and plains. As I ride along, three aspects of living become important with every turn of the pedals. Whether I ride through a country or across a continent, I'm meeting people and seeing the sights. For me, the most important thing is my connectedness, a combination of what I feel is important in keeping my life in relationship with the natural world, and therefore, myself—and that is—keeping my body, mind and spirit in balance.

I feel that life provides a moving drama that I enjoy exploring. A friend of mine, Duncan Littlefair said that when you walk forward, it's not that you walk forward, you fall forward, you're falling forward into the unknown, and the only thing that prevents you from falling down face first is that you put your other foot out and stop your fall, yet you continue to fall into the unknown with each step.

I think bicycling replicates that metaphor. I ride into each day having no idea what's going to happen. I ride with a positive attitude, and invariably, good things happen. It's rare that I ever ride into a negative situation—because life proves generally positive. Some people may complain that it's raining out today, so that's a negative. I don't see it that way. Rain makes flowers bloom. A mountain rises ahead. I have to drop into granny gear. It's a lot like anyone's life as they grow toward their own fulfillment. Each day, as I ride my bike into the unknown, the pedals move around in a constant rhythm of adaptation to the different kinds of terrain, and so do I, with my body, mind and spirit.

Starting with the body, a long-distance touring rider concerns himself or herself with health. That concern translates into taking care of your body. I exercise all the muscles, not just the ones for riding a bike because it's important to keep everything balanced.

My nutritional approach is vegetarian with an emphasis on raw natural foods—vegetables, fruits, nuts, grains. I compliment them with whole breads and pastas. I avoid meats and dairy products. This nutritional stance gives my body maximum clean burning fuel to push the pedals throughout the day. It makes me capable of responding to any physical needs whether it be hot, dry deserts such as the Atacama of Chile, the Outback of Australia, or a 15,000-foot pass in the Bolivian Andes. I can move through them with confidence because my body maintains a balance.

The five bodily senses play an important part of the day on a bicycle tour. I feel everything around me. I taste, touch, hear, smell and feel nature. I taste the rain on my tongue and touch the bark on a tree. I hear an owl hooting and smell a skunk. My senses soar because I am involved with the swirling forces of nature. I sweat in the desert and get chilled in the mountains. I am wild on my bicycle with the wind blowing past me.

Touring fills my mind with expectation. Something new awaits around the next bend in the road ahead. It can be confusing or frustrating. Most of the time, however, it's a positive experience. If you pinned me down, I would go with the word—serene. Nature creates inexplicable beauty. I love seeing it for the first time and my mind swallows it in big gulps.

Ultimately, my spiritual being moves through the natural world. I pedal, change gears, drink water, see an eagle, watch a storm, and sleep beneath the stars. These activities affect something deep down in my spirit. It's the balance in my life. It's something I can't really know, yet it seems to grow as I get older. It's a feeling inside me about life, which leaves me at peace with myself.

CHAPTER 29

Everything you need to know for long-distance bicycle adventure

"When I go biking, I repeat a mantra of the day's sensations: bright sun, blue sky, warm breeze, blue jay's call, ice melting and so on. This helps me transcend the traffic, ignore the clamorings of work, leave all the mind theaters behind and focus on nature instead. I still must abide by the rules of the road, of biking, of gravity. But I am mentally far away from civilization. The world is breaking someone else's heart." Diane Ackerman

GETTING STARTED

THE RIGHT BIKE

Everyone carries a bias about something dear to his or her heart. When it comes to bicycle touring, I've tried various approaches to equipment. Many of my lessons have been learned the hard way. Experience proves a stern taskmaster. I've stood in rainstorms with a breakdown, wondering why I hadn't listened to a friend who had been through it. Maybe I didn't listen because I thought I knew it all. Wrong! Even with miles and years behind my wheels, new ideas pop up daily. I'm willing to learn from other riders, because each one has a different style that incorporates something better into his or her bicycle touring operation.

Ben Franklin said it best: "Penny wise, pound foolish."

That wisdom holds true to this day. It applies to the bike you buy, and your gear.

More than once, I've been asked for advice on what kind of bike to ride. Am I biased? You bet. My inclination for bikes and equipment comes from a long trail of mistakes. You may obtain a host of experts' opinions, and they are valid relative to each person's needs, and aspirations in touring.

Light touring machine or heavy mountain bike?

Hands down—buy a mountain touring bike. It's the best thing to happen to bicycle touring either nationally or internationally. Cost? If you're touring plans mean two weeks per year in the USA, buy a bike in the $600.00 range. For international tours of six months duration, spend $1,500.00 or more and save money in the long run. For those who want the best, a custom-built mountain bike will cost $2,500.00 to $4,500.00. It's a lot of money and it's a lot of bicycle.

Some will tell you that a mountain bike is too heavy. Baloney. We're talking five pounds more at the most. That goes for women or men. You won't feel the weight. They say it handles harder. No way. Your body adapts to any load. That bike will become as comfortable as your favorite easy chair.

Excellent touring bikes: Kona, Salsa, Long Haul Trucker (Disc), Co-Motion, Franklin Frame and Diamond Back.

Why a mountain bike? First of all, comfort levels increase because of the fat tires. Buy ridged 1.75 tires for a smooth ride. A mountain bike offers a better, softer ride. You don't get front-end shimmy from being overloaded in the panniers or handlebar bag. Another big plus is the rarity of flat tires on a mountain bike. I've gone five months without a flat. No conventional touring bicycle can boast that. Those 1 1/4-inch tires get cut or worn out much too often. I love the security of knowing my tires are sturdy, especially on a long downhill, high-speed descent. Additionally, you can load a mountain bike up with tons of weight and not worry about spokes breaking (26-inch rim versus 700 rim "your wheel"), or wheels warping out of true. Best tire: Schwalbe Marathon Plus Tour.

Customize that mountain bike for touring. Replace the straight bars with wide drop bars or butterfly bars. That will give you three hand holding positions. Buy an aero bar that will give you a place to rest your forearms and take you over the front of the bike for hours of comfortable riding. That means your shifting levers must be relocated on the down tube, or bar end shifters are available. Install a 40-spoke rear wheel, if available, for added endurance, especially for international touring. Buy the heaviest gauge, highest quality spokes for that back wheel, and make certain the person who builds your wheel knows what he/she is doing. Check around and get several opinions. By investigating, you will discover the best bike person in your town. Be aware of fast talkers who seem to know it all. Ask them how much and where they have toured. Do they know how to fit a bike to your body? Make sure they do it. Learn how to do it yourself. It's important to get a perfect fit. Your enjoyment depends on it.

Two items in the drive train stand out as very important to me. I install a front Granny gear 24 tooth chain ring with a 34-tooth low end freewheel gear. No sense killing yourself on climbs. Best rear derailleur? I won't go anywhere without a Deore XT. That derailleur outlasts anything on the market.

You will develop your own style given a few miles, but it's nice to feel confident in your bicycle when you start out with a quality machine that fits your needs.

PREPARING FOR INTERNATIONAL BICYCLE TOURING

Going on a bicycle tour to some exotic country? Developing country? Whether you're going three weeks or six months, you have dozens of things to take care of before boarding the airplane. Preparing for an international tour is like battling a four-alarm fire. When you think one blaze is under control, another one needs immediate attention.

Begin preparing NOW—three to six months in advance. If you work forty or fifty hours a week, solid preparation will keep you from going crazy a week before departure. In my own world tours, I've found each continent needs specialized consideration. For example, in America, you can expect a bicycle shop in the next town if you need a spare part. In Africa, forget it. Whether you crank your bicycle across the Arctic Circle in Norway, push through the Andes Mountains in Peru, or sweat your way across the Nullarbor Plains of Australia—the success of your journey depends on what you do before you leave.

The key to that success is COMPLETION of your "To Do" and "To Buy" lists months before you leave. When you make your target date seven days to a month in advance of departure, you can relax at the bon voyage party without having an ulcer. Additionally, your health during the ride may depend on your advance preparation.

To make things easier on you, major and minor areas of concern will be covered. You may refer to "WHAT TO TAKE AND HOW TO PACK IT," in this chapter. As you begin to acquaint yourself with the enormity of international touring preparation, get out a pen and a paper, and start a list.

BICYCLE AND EQUIPMENT

Two to three-week guided tours usually enjoy a sag wagon and mechanics to repair and maintain your bicycle. With those tours, your bike, whether you rent or bring your own, is not as critical a factor in the success of your tour. However, buy a bike and gear that will serve you well, so you may ride in confidence. Before going on tour, a basic tune up is a must. If you buy a new bike, be sure to ride it 300 miles and have the wheels trued. Be certain to have the bike fitted to your body.

For persons riding into developing world countries, a mountain bike, (converted for touring by adding drop bars, 40 spoke hole rims, extra quart water bottle cages, anatomical touring seat, aero bar, lower gearing, and fenders added) is highly recommended. It not only offers a superior ride on gravel roads, the tires last longer with far fewer flats. Make sure the quality of the bike and components matches the length of your ride. Insist on sealed bearings, but if you can't buy them, make sure your hubs have been overhauled. Carry tools that work with every part of your bike. Take a course in bicycle repair.

Highly recommended: In the past several years, those 'aero' or 'Scott' bars have become vogue in racing circles because they lower the body resistance and create a bullet-like profile that is more streamlined. The big discovery for touring riders is a whole new form of comfort. By resting your arms on the bar, you rest your whole upper body and your butt. It allows for many more comfortable miles by taking the pressure off the triceps and shoulders. I highly recommend adding them to your comfort gear while on tour.

TENT, SLEEPING BAG, AIR MATTRESS AND COOKING GEAR

If you're on a guided tour, these items may not be important because lodging and food will be provided.

For those on individual tours, this equipment is extremely important. A quality, self-standing tent in the $250.00 to $350.00 range is a good bet. Be sure to seal the seams, carry extra seam sealer, and carry a waterproof ground mat.

A three-season sleeping bag at three pounds (down or fiberfill) good to 20 degrees Fahrenheit will keep you warm inmost conditions. If you get caught at high altitude, you may wear your tights, mittens, sweater and cap to bed for extra warmth. The BEST air mattress is a 3/4 length self-inflating Thermo-Rest by Cascade Designs. I buy my gear at www. REI.com www.LLBean.com, www.EMS.com, www.NorthFace.com because they give lifetime guarantees on their equipment.

Cooking gear includes a large pot, secondary pan, utensils, cups and a stove. Buy a stove that will burn many kinds of fuel for international destinations. An MSR International is one of the most popular and costs around $89.00. Talk with an REI employee for your specific needs and he/she will fill them. For the USA, a Coleman Primus with propane bottles works great.

DAY PACK OR SMALL BACK PACK

On top of your back rack, you may want to carry a 3,000 cubic inch capacity pack with three external pockets. It carries your tent, air mattress, ground tarp, flip flops and other gear.

Above the main pack, you can strap on a day pack for easy access to your camera, film, valuables and food. Carry your most often used gear in it. When stopping at a restaurant or whenever leaving the bike unattended for a few moments, you can release the bungee cords and sling the day pack over your shoulders.

Your tent, daypack and air mattress are the bulky pieces that must balance over the rear axle. Strap your tent forward under the seat. The air mattress will fit beside the tent. A second set of crossed bungee cords will secure your daypack. Check for hanging straps or bungee cords every time you finish packing your bike. Otherwise, you will wrap the around the freewheel or spokes. The results can tear up your wheel alignment or worse.

RAIN PROOFING YOUR GEAR

No doubt about it, you're at the mercy of the elements on a bicycle tour. Your equipment must be kept dry. Wrap everything in plastic bags. Keep your rain suit easily available. Make certain your film, digital cards and camera gear are securely rain proofed. Do the same for your sleeping bag and tent.

INTERNATIONAL TOURS

When riding in a foreign country, you're subject to different conditions. You may be vulnerable to infectious diseases, tainted food and water. You need extra precautions with eating, drinking and medicine. Boil, drop or filter your water, and eat only cooked foods. I use an MSR or First Need water filter. They are inexpensive and effective. Always peel fruits and vegetables. Wash your hands and keep your eating utensils clean. Drink only water you have filtered.

In a developing world country, you can expect a case of food poisoning at some point in your tour. Once you feel it coming on, induce yourself to vomit, and keep vomiting until your stomach is empty. Drink plenty of water to rinse out your system. This procedure will save you from prolonged suffering. If not food poisoning, you may pick up a new bacterium that doesn't agree with your intestines. In that case, you must tolerate the alien bugs until your system settles down to normal again.

Because you will not be able to bathe every day, carry anti-fungal ointment. Take a washcloth and wipe yourself down nightly with water. This will help prevent fungal growth on your skin. For poison ivy or skin rashes, carry Micatin cream. You can buy an MSR shower bag in order to take a three-minute shower every night.

Your passport is vulnerable to theft. Always keep it on your person or at arm's length.

IMMUNIZATION AND INOCULATIONS

Don't you love this category? It's a real pain in the rump, but necessary. Tell the nurse which countries you will be visiting and get your inoculations card completed with each shot or series. Take no chances with yellow fever, tetanus, typhoid, diphtheria or cholera. Insist on a Gamma Globulin shot for the best, but not perfect, prevention available for hepatitis. Tell them how long you intend to tour, so they can adjust the dosage accordingly. Seek out all information you need in this area, and act upon it. Call or write the Center for Disease Control, U.S. Department of Health and Human Services. The number is in your local phone book under U.S. Government. Or, look up on line! For shots, call your local hospital immunization department. If you demand answers, you will receive them. In this area, preparation and prevention are keys to your health.

Upon returning to the USA from a Developing world country, have a blood, urine and feces check to make sure you haven't picked up any liver flukes or other parasites. If tests are positive, begin treatment immediately.

In countries where malaria is present, you must start taking pills two weeks before leaving. With two or more people on the tour, take them on the same day, so everyone can remind each other during the ride. Follow instructions as your doctor tells you.

PASSPORT

This one can be a real hassle. Pick up the application at the post office. Fill it out and provide all documentation exactly as required. One mistake, and they will write you a letter with needed items for completion of your passport. In the meantime, your application is scattered between their office and your house.

Make certain you send them RECENT (within six months) official passport pictures and sign them on the back. Use those same pictures for visa applications. When applying for visas to different countries, use a travel agency's courier services. If you have any problems in processing, call your congressional representative. For peace of mind, make a list of the locations of American embassies in the countries you plan to visit.

Keep a dozen extra pictures for an international driver's license, hostel card and other needs that will pop up on an extended tour. Color, or black and white pictures are acceptable.

For extra precaution, take a photostat copy of your passport, driver's license and birth certificate. Put them in a separate compartment.

CAMERA EQUIPMENT

When the adventure ends, the pictures you snapped will be your most prized possessions. That is, if you didn't run the film through an airport x-ray machine, or soak the camera in a rainstorm, or forget a spare light meter battery.

Camera gear needs special attention, whether you carry an expensive digital mirrorless or a sure shot automatic. Keep your card in a waterproof bag and insist that airport security people hand inspect it. Always ride with your camera in a plastic bag and out of the sun. Carry a small tripod.

CUSTOMS

Before leaving the states, have customs officers document U.S. ownership of your bike, camera equipment, expensive jewelry and any other gear you consider worth claiming as previously purchased property. Otherwise, you could be liable for import taxes upon your return. Even more important, you could be charged more than $100.00 for an import tax in a developing world country!

NUTS AND BOLTS INFORMATION

Carry theft insurance for all your valuables overseas. Check with your insurance agent to make certain your bike and gear are covered.

Schedule a dental checkup and have everything in order before leaving. If you have a problem in a developing world country, you may suffer prolonged pain.

Money matters are very important. Purchase American Express traveler's checks because that company has the most offices throughout the world. Carry credit cards (Visa and Mastercard) that are honored internationally. Send your company $500.00 to $5,000.00 of debit credit, so you will have that to draw on if you're not back in time to pay a bill. You may need it in a pinch. Make certain their expiration date is after your return. ALWAYS keep them in your money belt. I keep my passport and valuables on my person 24 hours a day and within arm's reach when taking a shower. When sleeping in a hostel, stuff your valuables into the bottom of your sleeping bag. Camera gear can go into the closed end of your pillow case on your hostel sheet. NEVER assume your gear is safe from theft. It will be gone in seconds if left unattended.

For additional financial preparation, you can order foreign currency from your own bank. If you arrive in a country during a festival or other holiday, you will have at least $50.00 worth of their money for your immediate expenses.

If there is any question as to safety, write the embassy of the country you want to visit. I avoided Columbia completely on my tour through South America. Hostile guerrilla action broke out on the routes I had to take to get to Ecuador. My body is allergic to bullets and jail, so I never take any chances. For complete information from USA sources, call the Citizen's Adviser Center in Washington, D.C. at phone number (202) 647-5225; If a problem exists in a country, call (202) 647-6173; If a situation merits further investigation, call the Security Department, 24-hour command center at (202) 647-2412. Consider their suggestions seriously in your travel decisions.

Carry a booklet with addresses and phone numbers of embassies in a foreign country. Check in with the USA embassy staff and out when you leave a country.

DRUGS: Anyone who carries or consumes drugs in a foreign country is absolutely out of his or her mind. Jails in Developing world countries are loaded with Americans who thought they wouldn't get caught. I can't stress this enough: STAY AWAY FROM DRUGS OR ANYTHING THAT LOOKS, FEELS OR SOUNDS SUSPICIOUS. If someone traveling with you carries drugs, insist he or she gets rid of the contraband. If they refuse, separate yourself from them. You may be considered an accomplice. Police in developing world countries lock you up and throw away the key.

Purchase your plane tickets two or three months in advance for possible discount prices, and assurance that you have a plane seat. Shop for an airline that charges least for a bicycle as extra baggage. Some airlines charge $150.00 for your bicycle ONE WAY.

Break your bike down and pack it in a sturdy box. Be sure to secure the front forks by placing a block of wood in the axle and tape it in place. Unscrew the rear derailleur from the dropout. Tape it to the chain inside some paper or a rag. That will save it from being bent. Or, have a shop do it for you. But, you must know how to reconstruct your bike at destination, so learn how to break it down and put it back together.

Learn a few valuable phrases in the language of the country(s) you may visit. Learn to say "Hello, goodbye, good morning, good night, where is the toilet? How much? Yes, no, Mr., Mrs., please and thank you."

Carry a phrase book to help you along. People will warm up when you try to speak their language.

If you won't get back before April 15th, you need to fill out a Federal Income tax extension form. By proving you were out of the country, you have an automatic 90-day extension (you can show a copy of your airline ticket). However, you must have enough paid into the IRS in order not to suffer penalties.

If someone is taking care of your house, or you are renting it out, you need to fill out a Power of Attorney form giving someone you trust the legal right to handle your personal affairs, such as eviction of destructive renters or those who bounce rent checks. Leave that person with extra funds to pay for emergency or unexpected bills.

Fill out a will and register it in probate court. Notify your benefactor. It costs less than $10.00 to register.

Make sure your insurance payments are in order. Car, house, bike and any other insured items must have up-to-date premiums paid.

Carry a travel handbook that gives you the in's and out's of each country and major cities. Carry a Youth Hostel book with locations and phone numbers.

Today, with smart phones, you enjoy 24/7 connections to the world. However, you may need mail at some point.

Leave a travel itinerary with loved ones of post office addresses in major cities. Tell them to address the envelope with your name, c/o Poste Restante, Central Post Office, City and Country. Poste Restante is the international word for general delivery. You can pick up your mail at a post office by showing your passport. Tell your friends to write to each address three weeks in advance of the tentative dates you have written down on your itinerary. If you're not sure where you will be and don't want to write all your friends each time with a possible new address, you can have your friends write to one address in the states at your best friend's or parent's house and have your mail forwarded from there. It's easier that way. I can tell you that letters are like Christmas gifts, and mean so much when you are a long way from home.

Another nice communication mode is 'hotmail' on the computer. You can pick up email virtually around the world today. You dial up your personal code and you can write and read letters to and from your friends. Check with any carrier to get hooked up.

Carry the international dialing phone number of your local bicycle shop. If you suffer a major breakdown, they can express mail you a replacement. By keeping stocked with parts from the pack list, you should be covered.

When traveling through multiple countries, you must have a plane ticket home, and enough money to show you are financially responsible while touring that country. Otherwise, authorities may not let you enter their country.

Check with your travel agent to see if you need a visa for a particular country, or whether they give an automatic 30 day visa. Once you arrive in a country that has granted you an automatic visa, but you didn't obtain one for the next country you will visit—you can apply at the embassy in the capitol of the country you are now touring. Remember to take extra pictures.

Always be cordial and smile. Be as neat and clean as you can, and act respectfully toward authorities.

For anyone going on a long-distance tour, buy a special padded seat cover with the latest in silicone cushioning. It will save your rear end. For double insurance, seats now offer this material and you can add the cover for ultimate comfort.

PHYSICAL CONDITIONING

Your physical preparation is one of the most important keys to enjoyment while on tour. Ride your bike every day for a month before departure. If you're headed into the mountains, find some steep grades where you live, and ride them with your loaded panniers. If none exist, ride a high resistance stationary bike at the local health club.

If you fail to prepare your legs, a slight strain or ligament pull will finish you abruptly on a bicycle adventure because it will get worse with every added mile. Make sure you avoid that: get into pedaling shape.

BIKE SECURITY

Your bike security at night or while visiting a monument is important. Either check into a safe hotel where you can keep the bike in your room (I cable it to a pipe or anything secure), or have someone in your party stay with the cycles and gear. Lock the bikes to something solid and keep equipment in your tent at night.

One point on safety: cut a fiberglass bicycle safety flagpole to three feet. Push it through the bungee cords on the rear of your pack so that it sticks two feet out to the traffic side in whatever country you're touring. This technique keeps drivers from scaring the heck out of you because it forces them to pass at a safer distance, or wait to pass at a better time. For added safety, I fly another orange flag, hose clamped to the rear rack, eight feet up vertically.

ATTITUDE

Patience: In developing world countries, during any situation, remain calm, patient and respectful. Learn to accept their ways, even though they may be frustrating, and different from your own.

One last point on international bicycle touring—you are pedaling into strange lands, meeting new people and experiencing different cultures. You will have the time of your life. Leave excess baggage like prejudice, discrimination and discourtesy at home. Stretch your emotional, mental and spiritual wings to learn about the world. Ride as a personal ambassador from your country. The impressions you make on people will remain with them forever. Share a smile, kind words and good things will come your way.

Enjoy a grand bicycle adventure in good health and high spirits.

WHAT TO TAKE AND HOW TO PACK IT

One of the most frustrating feelings on a bicycle tour is when you dig into your pack for something and can't find it. Even worse is realizing you didn't bring it. It can be as small as a pair of tweezers or as important as a spoke wrench. The best way to prevent such a calamity is to keep a pack list that you can check off before leaving for your adventure.

Special precautions must be taken in five areas each time you load your gear into your panniers. When you need an item, you want it easily available. That goes double for your first aid kit.

International tours require extra attention to details, and at least three months advance preparation.

EQUIPMENT ORGANIZATION

Organizing your equipment is the best way to have it ready for your use. If it's small, light and you use it often, the best storage place is a zipper pouch on the rear panniers or your daypack. Depending on how you stand your bike, items used often need to be on the free side of the bike. For efficiency, group common items like a toothbrush and soap in the same nylon 'ditty' bags. These drawstring pouches are handy. You can use clear plastic bags to separate clothes into organized compartments. You can do the same for tire repair tools.

When your gear is packed, especially on your first trip, it takes a few days of rearranging everything to place it where you like. Once that's accomplished, draw a schematic of where everything is placed. Use it for quick reference when packing for future rides.

WEIGHT DISTRIBUTION

The first rule in bicycling touring is: If you don't need or use it, leave it. Why? Simple—weight adds up quickly. Every excess pound you pack will cost you in bike stability and miles covered daily. When riding with four panniers, you need to pack the heaviest equipment— like stove, fry pan, and cable lock—into the lowest sections of your rear panniers. That will keep your "lean" weight closer to the ground. Lean weight means the amount of weight you have on the bike and where it is located. If you pack heavy items higher up in the panniers, the bike will be top heavy.

When loading your bicycle, you need to balance weight from side to side. More weight should be in the rear panniers than in the front. If you experience a shimmy in your handlebars, it means you have too much in your handlebar bag. Keep less than four pounds in it. If a shimmy persists, lighten your front panniers and check the side to side balance. Traditional touring bikes with light frames and skinny tires have a shimmy problem more than touring mountain bikes. That's why I recommend a mountain bike for touring.

CAMERA EQUIPMENT CARE

Keep your camera equipment in plastic bags at all times. While on tour, dust swirls around you from cars and the wind. Also, you must be concerned about rain. Large zip lock freezer bags work well, and you can see through them and reuse them. Keep camera gear in the daypack cushioned over your sleeping bag and air mattress rolls.

DAYPACK AND INTERNAL FRAME BACK PACK

A small daypack will keep many of your valuables safe and ready for use. They are as handy as any book pack that you used back in school. It'll carry your camera and valuable gear that you want with you at a moment's notice.

A 2,000 to 3,000 cubic inch internal frame pack with three side compartments is an excellent addition to your versatility while on tour. You can store your air mattress, gear, along with extra digital cards, valuables and food. Make it the easy access pack to your most often used gear. If you happen to find yourself in a backpacking situation, you're ready to go.

RAINPROOFING YOUR GEAR

No doubt about it, you're at the mercy of the elements on a bicycle tour. Your equipment must be kept dry. Wrap everything each morning in plastic bags. Keep your rain suit available. Make certain your camera gear is rain proofed. Do the same for your sleeping bag and tent.

NIGHT LIGHT IN YOUR TENT

Miner's lamps cost $20.00 and will give you ample light for writing in the tent or cooking dinner outside.

CYCLING SHOES, GLOVES, GLASSES, SHORTS AND HELMET

Buy the best, most comfortable cycling shoes you can afford. Do not ride with tennis shoes. You need the plastic or steel shank on the bottom of the shoes to give you protection from the pedals. Without that shank, you will be in a lot of pain and cause your legs to waste a lot of energy to compensate.

Buy a good pair of cycling gloves to protect you from pounding your hands to death. The first week of a cycling trip, keep shaking your hands at regular intervals so you won't crush the ulnar nerve in the palm of the hand. If you have 'aero' bars, you will be able to give your hands a rest. That bar will take the pressure off your ulnar nerve. I highly recommend it.

With the ozone vanishing, you need to buy 100% UV glasses to stop damage to your eyes. I wear the very best eye protection. I buy the sunglasses with leather side blocks to protect you from the wind and they have a cord to keep them around your neck.

Buy two pairs of cycling shorts, either regular touring shorts or Lycra. Make sure you buy the suede-padded shorts instead of leather because sued is easier to wash and wear. If you are riding in extremely sunny weather, you might want to wear thin Thermax protection in the form of a shirt that covers your arms and neck. If it's blistering sunshine, wear thin tights to protect your legs from hours of radiation from the sun. A tan looks nice, but the damage to your skin accumulates into wrinkles, and potential skin cancers. Your body does not need all that sun. Protect your face daily with maximum sun block.

Always wear a helmet. Two people on average per day die in the USA while riding a bicycle each year. Over 50,000 persons visit hospitals with broken bones and cuts bad enough to need medical attention after bike crashes each year. The most serious accidents are head injuries because people weren't wearing helmets. For touring, be certain to buy a visor on your helmet for sun protection. They can stitch you up, and they can set your broken bones—but they can't pour your brains back into your head the right way. Wear a helmet. If the helmet doesn't have a visor, you can buy one at a motorcycle shop and drill new holes and fit it on yourself.

INTERNATIONAL TOURING

Any time you ride into a foreign country; you're subject to different conditions. You may be vulnerable to infectious diseases, tainted food and water. You need extra precautions with eating, drinking and medicine. Boil, use drops or filter your water, and eat only cooked foods. Always peel fruits and vegetables. You might consider becoming a temporary vegetarian once you see how dairy products and meats are left out in the sun with flies crawling everywhere.

Because you will not be able to bathe every day, carry an antifungal ointment. Take a wash cloth and wipe yourself down nightly with water from your bottles. This will help prevent fungal growth on your skin. For poison ivy or other skin rashes, carry Micatin cream.

Your passport is vulnerable to theft. ALWAYS keep it and money on your person, in a pouch around your neck or in your pack. Your daypack should always go with you on a break, or have a trusted friend watch the gear while you go to the restroom.

During a tour in foreign countries, preventive maintenance is very important. Check your spokes often and take plenty of spare nuts and bolts. Two spare tubes and one extra tire are a minimum. Carry enough patch gear for 20 punctures. You will need a freewheel puller wrench, chain breaker and rear derailleur. In developing world countries, strongly consider a mountain bike converted for touring, i.e., put drop bars on it, 'aero' bars, and ride with 1.75 tires with a 40 spoke 26-inch rim. For heavily mountainous countries, try a 24 front 'Granny' gear chain ring to a 34 teeth rear freewheel or cassette climbing gear.

FUEL BOTTLE AND GEAR PLACEMENT

You will find your own style for placing equipment. However, the fuel bottle is a potentially troublesome item. Some riders place it in their lower water bottle clip on the down tube. You can wrap it in plastic and set it upright in the rear pouch of your panniers. In either case, be certain to secure the opening from leakage. This pack list may be customized to suit you. Use or discard items as you need them for yourself.

PACKING LIST

TOP OF FRONT PANNIER RACK

1. Sleeping Bag and Silk Cocoon in Water Proof Stuff Sack
2. Grey Handlebar Bag
    1. Front of Bike White Light (3 AAA)
    2. Rear of Bike LED Red Warning Light (2 AAA)
    3. Chamois Cream
    4. Tire Pressure Gauge
    5. Riding Carb Fuel
    6. Eyeglass Cleaning Liquid & Cloth
    7. Sunglass Case W/Reg. Glasses
    8. SPF 100 Sun Block
    9. SPF 50 Chap Stick
    10. Hand Sanitizer
    11. Swiss Army Knife
    12. Mobile Phone

13. Camera, extra digital cards
14. Travel Wallet

LEFT FRONT PANNIERS ('B')

1. Instant Oatmeal
2. Hot Drink Mixes (tea, coffee, hot chocolate)
3. Peanut Butter
4. Bread or Tortillas
5. Three One-Gallon Freezer Bags
6. Three One-Quart Freezer Bags
7. Three One-Pint Freezer Bags
8. Riding Carb Fuel (Dried Fruit, Apples, Bananas, Oranges)
9. Stuff Sack with Energy Bars
10. Sports Drink Mix

RIGHT FRONT PANNIER ('A')

1. Spice Shaker
2. Vegetable Broth Cubes
3. Dinner Staples (Pasta, Lentils, Couscous, Quinoa, Etc.)
4. Dehydrated Evening Meals
5. Salad Fixings
6. Extra Riding Carb Fuel (Dried Fruit, Apples, Bananas, Oranges)

RIGHT REAR PANNIER ('D')

1. Outside Pocket
   1. First Aid Kit
   2. Folding Water Container

2. 0.6L Fuel Bottle in Freezer Bag
3. 325mL Fuel Bottle W/Pump
4. MSR 2.0 L Pot w/Strainer Lid
   1. Brunton Cook Stove
   2. Dish Towel

3. Matches
4. Pot Gripper
5. Fork
6. Liquid Soap
7. Scouring Pad

5. Snow Peak Individual Cook Set, MSR cook set, you decide for your needs
   1. 0.8 L Cooking Pot
   2. Lid
   3. 10 oz. Cup

6. Gallon Freezer Bag
   1. Plate
   2. Long Handled Spoon
   3. Long Handled Knife
   4. Stove Wind Shield

7. Repair Kit
   1. Assorted Bandages
   2. 2 Tire Irons
   3. Open End Wrenches, 7-10 Mm
   4. Allen Wrenches, All Sizes to Fit Bike
   5. Leatherman Squirt Pliers
   6. 6" Adjustable Wrench
   7. Chain Tool
   8. Three Grease Rags
   9. Nuts, Bolts (Assorted)
   10. Chain Links
   11. One Tire Patch Kit (6-8 Patches)
   12. Brake Cable
   13. Gear Cable
   14. Brake Blocks
   15. 4 – 6" Plastic Tie Straps
   16. Short Length Elect. Tape

17. 26 X 1.5 – 1.75 Presta Valve Tube
18. Tent Seam Sealer

LEFT REAR PANNIER ('C')

1. Outside Pocket
   1. Clothes Drying Net Bag
   2. Insect Repellent
   3. Cable and Combination Lock
   4. Chain Lube, Grease Rag & Small Tube of Grease Remover Hand Cleaner in Plastic Bag

2. Street Clothes Stuff Sack
   1. 1 – PR. Lt. Wt. Long Pants w/zippered Legs
   2. 1 – Lt. Wt. Long Sleeve Shirt w/roll up sleeves
   3. 1 – Pr. Lt. Wt. Underwear
   4. 1 – T Shirt
   5. 1 - Swim Suit

3. Bike Wear Stuff Sack
   1. 1 – Pr. Biking Socks
   2. 1 - Thermax Long Sleeve Jersey
   3. 1 - Thin Sun Protection Long Sleeve Jersey
   4. 1 – Pr. Riding Shorts
   5. 1 – Pr. Biking Tights

4. Cold Weather Stuff Sack
   1. 1 - Under Armor Top
   2. 1 - Under Armor Bottom
   3. 1- Stocking Cap

5. Shower Sandals in Net Bag
6. Toiletry Kit
   1. 30 Days Flaxseed
   2. 30 Days Aspirin

3. 30 Days Glucosamine W/MSM
4. 30 Days One-A-Day Vitamin
5. Sewing Kit
6. Gore-Tex Repair Kit
7. 1 – Disposable Razor
8. Tooth Paste
9. Toothbrush
10. Dental Floss
11. Comb
12. Travel Wallet Contents List

7. Small Net Bag
    1. Microfiber Towel
    2. Deodorant Bar Soap in Plastic Bag

TOP OF REAR PANNIER RACK

1. Duffle Bag, preferably oblong and squared off
    1. Rain Protection Plastic Bag W/Closure Device
    2. Tent in Stuff Sack
    3. Poles in Stuff Sack
    4. Ground Cloth & Rain Fly in Stuff Sack
    5. 14 Tent Stakes in Bag (1 Extra)
    6. Air Mattress in Stuff Sack
    7. Lightweight Camping Chair
    8. Plastic Bag for Bicycle Seat Rain Cover
    9. 30' Of Nylon Cord
    10. Mini Clothes Pins

2. Red & Black Daypack
    1. Rain Cover Plastic Bag W/Velcro Strap Closure
    2. Rain Jacket

    3. Rain Gear Stuff Sack
        1. Rain Pants

2. Rain Booties
3. Helmet Cover
4. Gloves

4. Gallon Plastic Freezer Bag
   1. Gear Location Schematic
   2. Maps
   3. Bike Specs.

5. Zippered Pocket
   1. Night LED Head Light (3 AAA)
   2. Ear Plugs
   3. SPF 50 Chap Stick
   4. Nighttime Eye Cover
   5. Spare Batteries
      1. 3 - AAA
      2. Camera

6. One Roll Camper Toilet Paper in Plastic Bag
7. Small Net Bag
   1. Phone Charger
   2. Camera Battery Charger

8. Quart Freezer Bag
   1. Postcard Stamps
   2. Journal
   3. Address List

9. Two Pens
10. Two carabineers on Outside of pack
11. Water purification tablets

REMOVABLE BIKE ACCESSORIES

1. Frame Mounted Air Pump
2. 3 Water Bottles

3. Handlebar Mount Warning Bell
4. Rear View Mirror
5. Two 14" Bungee Cords
6. Four 20" Bungee Cords
7. One 11" Bungee Cord
8. One Short 27" Safety Flag
9. One Long 6' Safety Flag
10. Two Parking Brake 11" Velcro Straps
11. Bike Computer (1 Cr 2032 + 1 12v)
12. 3 Spokes with Nipples Mounted on Left Chain Stay
13. Two Extra Halo Sweat Bands on Aero Bars

WEARING TO RIDE

1. Helmet
2. Halo Sweat Band
3. Sunglasses
4. Short Sleeve Bike Jersey
5. Bike Shorts
6. Bike Socks
7. Bike Shoes
8. Bike Gloves
9. Riding Food in Jersey Pockets
10. Hydration Pack

NEEDED (make yourself a 'need to buy' list)

1. Long Handled Peanut butter Spreading Knife 8" REI Campware Knife
2. Adjustable nylon webbing straps instead of bungee cords
3. Better Velcro straps to attach grey handlebar bag to sleeping bag and front pannier rack
4. Ink marker for tire tube to mark leak

On departure day pack added

1. Lip Balm
2. Bike Repair Book
3. Camera Instructions
4. Destination Tour Book
5. Blanket & Pillow
6. Toiletry Kit
7. Sunglass Case W/Sunglasses
8. Eye Cover for Sleeping
9. Riding Clothes
10. Riding Shoes
11. Bike Computer
12. Radio w/earphone

On Departure Day Pack Deleted (again, use as backup)

1. One Roll Toilet Paper
2. Trowel
3. Packable Broad Brim Hat

Travel Clothing

1. Long Pants
2. Long Sleeve Shirt
3. North Face Shoes
4. Normal Socks
5. Poly Underwear
6. Prescription Glasses

Ship Back – UPS (You may want to ship gear back to lighten load, example)

1. North Face Shoes
2. Normal Socks
3. 2 Duffel Bags

4. Blanket and Pillow
5. Eye Cover for Sleeping
6. Radio w/earphone
7. Tool Kit stuff
    1. Straight Blade Screw Driver
    2. Side Cutters

MAIL BACK ON LEAVING DESTINATION CITY OR COUNTRY

1. Tour Book
2. Bike Repair Book
3. Camera Instruction

First Aid Kit

1. 6 -10 4x4" Pads for Cleaning Wound and Soaking Blood
2. 4 - 6 4x4" Non-Stick Pads for Covering Wound
3. 1 – 2" Ace Stretch Wrap
4. 1 Triangular Arm Sling
5. 4-8 Large Safety Pins
6. 4-6 Bandage Strips With 2 To 3 Inch Square Pads
7. Tape, 1 Inch Wide, Surgical Tape (3-6 Yards or Meters).
8. 6-10 Packets Or 1 Small 2-3 Oz. Bottle of Wound Sanitizer/Cleaner Betadine, Hibiclens, Peroxide, Baby Wipes or Soap and Water
9. 1 Small Tube Triple Antibiotic Salve for Dressing Cuts and Abrasions
10. 1 Small Tube, Hydrocortisone, 1% Or 2.5%, Topical Usage Only. Reduces Inflammation, Rashes, Saddle Sores and Allergic Reactions.
11. 10-20 Tablets/Capsules Tylenol, *Acetaminophen*: For Muscle and Body Pain, Joint Pain, Headaches, Fever, Allergies, Cough, Cold, And Flu
    1. 10-20 Tablets/Capsules Motrin Or Advil, *Ibuprofen*: Anti-Inflammatory, Pain Killer
    2. 5-10 Tablets/Capsules Benadryl, *Diphenhydramine Hydrochloride*: General Anesthetic, Antihistamine, Anti Swelling, Sleeping Pill,

Sedative, Anti Bleeding - Called: Nuprin, Medipren, Brufen, Anti-Vomiting/Nausea, Motion Sickness

1. 3-4 Band Aids ½" Wide (1.5 Cm & 2.5 Cm Wide), Keep Some in Tool Kit, In Small Plastic Bag
2. 3-4 Band Aids 1" Wide (1.5 Cm & 2.5 Cm Wide), Keep Some in Tool Kit, In Small Plastic Bag
3. Moleskin- Prevent Blister
4. Molefoam – Protect Blister
5. Solarcaine -Sunburn Relief
6. Imodium Ad- Anti-Diarrheal
7. Visine - Eye Irritation
8. Eucerine - Moisturizing Lotion
9. Rolaids - Anti-Acid
10. Lotromin Af - Anti Fungal
11. Calamine - Sting / Itch Relief

Safety and extras for national and international travel

1. Take a six-foot, fiberglass orange/lime green flag pole, lock to back rack.
2. Take a three-foot, fiberglass orange/lime green traffic side flag pole, bungee into traffic side.
3. Two extra tires, two extra tubes, 20 patches.
4. One extra chain.
5. Extra rear derailleur.
6. Extra freewheel or rear cassette.
7. Passport, shot records, international driver's license, Scuba Diving Card, extra passport sized pictures, hostel card, silk sheet for sleeping bag, bird book, Frisbee (optional), Hacky sack, snake bite kit, 30 feet of nylon cord, spare toe clip, extra nuts, washers and bolts, toe clip strap, swimmer's goggles, malaria pills, small binoculars, metric conversion card, bear repellant spray.
8. When traveling on a train, boat or plane, make sure you buy a NEW fuel bottle and mark it a 'water' bottle with duct tape. If the TSA

people try to confiscate it, and they will, put some water in it and drink it to show them. Otherwise, they will take it away from you, and you will be without a fuel bottle when you reach South America or Africa or some other place.

9. Spare brake cable, spare gearing cable, spare brake pads, spare pulley, photo copies of passport, driver's license, sewing kit, MSR stove cleaner and repair kit, birth certificate copy, water purification tablets, suture and thread, folding gallon container, spare spokes front and back, spare reading glasses, chain oil, chain breaker, freewheel cog remover, spare ball bearings, bottom bracket puller, pocket vice, crank remover, crazy glue, valve stem remover, swim suit, cable and combination lock.

INTERNATIONAL TOURING RECOMMENDATIONS

When riding outside the grocery-store-and-fast-food borders of the United States, you open yourself up to new culinary challenges and dangers. In America, you can count on clean water. The U.S. Department of Agriculture inspects meats. Most people speak English. You enjoy smooth roads and easy living.

You're sick of it, right? Too many motor home mentalities! Cable TV hookups in campsites! Every town in America looks like every other town. First you see the Golden Arches, followed by Wendy's, Subway, Arby's and Pizza Hut. Everyone walking out of a fast-food restaurant looks like they need special coaching from Jenny Craig and the TV program: Biggest Losers! Ye gads! Whatever happened to regional flavor, small town diners, personal dress and style? Does anyone remember what an old-time hardware store smells like? Do they know the wooden floors creak? Not a chance!

Sounds like you're ready to see how the other 95 percent lives. Hold onto your handlebars and pull up your Lycra shorts because you're in for one heck of a surprise. You face amazing sights and experiences in the developing world.

Always be aware of your potential circumstances on tour in developing countries. Be smart! Be prudent! Be prepared! Your life may depend on your thoughtful and measured actions. You cannot hope someone will rescue you like they do in the movies.

Anytime you ride into a foreign country, you're subject to conditions you won't find at home. You may be vulnerable to infectious diseases, tainted food and contaminated water. You need extra precautions with eating, drinking and medicine.

Riding Outside the United States

While on tour in any one of more than 190 countries, give or take a revolution every five years, you will notice many differences. The freedoms you take for granted at home may be turned upside down in other countries. The way people dress on the altiplano, treeless land above 12,000 feet in Bolivia, is different from the natives in Bali. People in the Middle East bow to Allah five times a day and the women are covered except for their eyes. Australia's kangaroos may enthrall you with their 40-foot leaps. Europe's architecture and history will seduce you. The cultures, languages, animals and people you visit will change dramatically from country to country. Your patience and understanding will be challenged often in foreign lands.

Please enjoy that people around the world offer smiles and friendships. They laugh, cry and struggle through different parts of their lives, just like you do. You travel through the 'village' of humanity.

Along the way, you need to adapt. That 'adaptation' keys your success. When it comes to eating, you face challenges and fabulous experiences.

First, you face a 90 percent certainty of suffering from food poisoning or bacterial disruption of your stomach and colon. Whether it's giardia cysts, worms, dysentery, hepatitis or food poisoning—you're headed for the bathroom. The key: accept its inevitability, treat it, endure it and get on with your tour. Take along medicine for diarrhea and pills to kill parasites. Get those medications in your doctor's office.

Water on International Tours

The primary concern on international tours: water! The rule remains simple:

12. Always filter your water.
13. Use purification tablets to ensure saety.

Make certain when you're filtering water to avoid mixing droplets of unfiltered water with filtered water. Just one unfiltered or untreated droplet can cause you sickness. That's why a purification tablet gives you a second line of defense in making your water safe.

No matter how much time it takes to filter water, do it painstakingly. It can mean the difference between miles of smiles and days of lying on your back with giardia making your colon feel like it's an arena for a bumper-car rally.

Diseases

Several diseases await you while on tour in developing countries. Be prudent and you will save yourself from most of them. Take every preventative shot in the book to protect yourself. Your physician can provide immunizations for you.

Hepatitis causes one heck of a lot of misery in developing countries. To combat it, take gamma-globulin shots that last up to six months. So far, so good! Make sure you take the shot several weeks before the trip, and avoid taking a gamma-globulin shot with any live virus vaccines. Your doctor will know about that.

If you contract hepatitis, you will feel like someone used your body as a practice target for a bow and arrow. You will be weak, your eyes will turn yellow, and your urine will darken.

You can contract hepatitis from food or water. If you come down with it, see a doctor as quickly as possible.

The Inca Two-Step, or Montezuma's Revenge, or Buddha's Belly give you an idea of 'bowel affliction' called diarrhea in the United States. You will spend entire days on the toilet and your face in the lavatory! If you discover blood in your feces, along with cramps in your stomach, it could be dysentery. You may need to take tetracycline. See a doctor.

Upon returning from any international tour, have your feces, blood and urine checked for bugs.

Food Transport Over Long Distances

One of your biggest challenges will be transporting food and water across long stretches of desert or uninhabited mountains. Be sure to look at a map and find out how far it is to the next food and water. We have carried as much as six days of food with us when we rode from La Paz, Bolivia to Arica, Chile. Our bikes looked more like pack mules than touring machines.

Our supplies included 10 days' worth of oatmeal, dried beans and rice, dried breads and rolls, tuna, dried fruit, potatoes, carrots and onions, and other sturdy, non-perishable foods. With rice and beans, and oatmeal—you can enjoy protein and carbs to power you anywhere.

In desert situations, like the Atacama Desert of Chile, or the Sahara in Africa, you're looking at hundreds of miles of sand. You won't see a fly or mosquito. You will need to bring four gallons of water with you to ensure making it to the next road house. That's especially important on the Nullarbor Plains (treeless) in the Outback of Australia, where temperatures exceed 120 degrees Fahrenheit and higher. The sun sucks water out of your skin like a wet-vac vacuum. I've toured 100 miles in Death Valley at 116 degrees F, 190 degrees at ground level. I have downed five gallons in one day, and never hit the bathroom!

Preventative maintenance and health on tour

Because you will not be able to bathe every day, carry antifungal ointment. Or, take a 1.5 gallon 'shower bag' with you offered at most camping stores. You can rinse down, soap up, and rinse off within three minutes. Just hang the bag on a tree and, voila, you're clean for sleeping. Great invention! Still carry the anti-fungal ointment! Also carry cortisone cream for poison ivy.

During a tour anywhere, preventative maintenance: very important! Check your spokes and screws daily to make sure they are tight. Gear ratio: 24 to a 34-rear granny! No need to bust your guts when you can spin with ease!

There's a reason you're traveling along adventure highway. As John Muir wrote, "Camp out among the grass and gentians of glacier meadows, in craggy garden nooks full of Nature's darlings. Climb the mountains and get their good tidings. Nature's peace will flow into you as sunshine flows into trees. The winds will blow their freshness into you, and the storms their energy, while cares will drop off like autumn leaves."

Be smart. Stay prepared. Enjoy the peace and silence. It's all good!

Baker's Dozen Suggestions

You will develop dozens of personal habits while touring. Your gear will be placed where you want it and you will evolve an almost ritualistic style of doing things.

Of course, the most important think you can do is buy a good bike and have a touring veteran fit it to your body. Have the bike fitted at four junctures:

14. Fit the right sized bike for your height.
15. Fit your seat to pedal height. With your shoe heel at 6:00 o'clock position while sitting in the seat, have someone hold you straight,

you need to have a 10 percent bend in the knee. This will give you maximum pedal, muscle and power coordination.

16. Fit your knee to your pedal axle. You should be able to drop a plumb line straight from the back of your patella to the axle of the pedal. Adjust your seat to make sure you're exactly in line with your patella and the axle for a perfect fit and comfort.

17. Fit the length from your seat to your handlebars. A general rule of thumb is to push your elbow from the tip of the seat and you longest middle finger will touch the handlebars for a perfect riding angle and fit. Go to a professional bike shop to get it done for you if you are unsure.

I would buy a bike from a good bicycle store where you will enjoy good service after the sale. If you buy mail order, be sure you know that you're doing or have a friend who knows what he or she is going to help you select the best bike.

Here's that Baker's Dozen ideas:

18. No matter how much you ride, someday you will take a fall. Since you don't know how bad the fall will be, you must anticipate the worst and wear a helmet. About 2.5 Americans die daily from falling off bicycles. That's 900 a year. Most of them cracked their heads like an egg yolk and didn't live. About 50,000 suffer broken bones, cuts and other injuries. Wear your helmet so you don't become a statistic. Buy and ANSI approved helmet and strap it on every time you get on your bicycle!

19. Buy the best sunglasses you can afford to protect your eyes. Protect yourself from deadly radiation from constant sun burning down on your face and body.

20. Buy an excellent pair of shoes designed specifically for bicycle riding with steel or plastic shank along the foot bed to give your even pressure and comfort. Without a good shoe, your food will feel more pressure pain than you can imagine. Check www.performance.com ; www.bikenashbar.com ; www.REI.com.

21. Learn how to maintain and repair your bicycle. Take a bicycle repair class with hands-on instruction. You need to be able to take apart your head tube, hubs, bottom bracket and freewheel or cassette assembly. If you're on a world tour, you need to be able to true your wheels and possibly rebuild a rim! You must know how to repair a tube or save a tire with 'duct tape' to the side walls to get more mileage when you're in a remote village in South America. Take the tools you need and know how to use them.

22. Your nutrition on a bike trip is important. Stay as close to high carbohydrates and simple proteins as possible for maximum efficiency. You will gain more stamina, power and endurance from pasta, grains, fruits, cereals, vegetables and breads. You may want to take multiple vitamins on an extended tour for 'added' nutrition. Your body suffers considerable depletion of resources while pedaling days on end.

23. Also, in order to defend against skin cancer, cover your body with long sleeve jersey and tights and hood down from your helmet to protect your ears and neck. Use 50 block sunscreen and lip balm.

24. Drink liquids constantly. Water provides the best drink on tour.

25. While touring in high mountains, allow your body to acclimate itself to the altitude. If not, you could suffer from altitude sickness. If you push too hard, too fast, you could suffer from pulmonary edema. If you feel weak, short of breath and start coughing, drop below 10,000 feet and stay there for a few days until you feel well enough to climb again. Cerebral edema is a more serious sickness because it affects your brain. You will suffer a pounding headache and possible double vision. If you do not act, death could result. Descend to below 10,000 feet and get medical attention.

26. When taking airlines and trains to major destinations, you will have to box your bike for transport. Visit a bicycle shop and pick out a box that fits your bike, or ask them to save you one, or check out their dumpster for extra boxes. Learn how to break your bike down and put it back together so you won't depend on a bike shop.

27. You will attract lots of attention while touring and many people will invite you into their homes. I have never encountered a problem,

but you need to be cautious, especially if you are a woman. You might accept lodging only if you meet a family or couple. I would shy away from single men asking you over to stay the night. Also, many men enjoy a faster cadence and move ahead of their women partners. This is important: if you're on tour with your wife or a female companion, ride behind her so you stay together. If you pedal too far ahead, she will feel alone and vulnerable. She will be highly agitated given enough time, and your relationship will suffer—along with your tour. Trust me on this one, guys!

28. Dogs can be the bane of your bicycling tour. They will frighten the daylights out of you and worse, bite you. You could be sent to the hospital for stitches or rabies shots. If a dog or dogs attack, they usually bark first so you know they are coming. It's worth your efforts to deal with their attacks quickly. Always be alert for dogs by keeping an eye on a house or any areas you think houses dogs. If you can outrun dogs by pedaling past their territory, go for it. You can carry a dog repellant spray, or better yet, pull your traffic side three-foot-long fiberglass safety pole out from under your bungee cords and show it to them by waving it back and forth. That 'whip' will calm them down quickly and they will leave you alone. If pressed, carry a few stones in your handlebar bag and throw them at the dogs. Carry wasp & hornet spray in a can with a 30-foot stream. Aim at their faces. As a last resort, dismount your bike and walk behind it as you move out of their territory.

29. Always be prepared for survival situations by carrying ample water, food and shelter. Carry minimum amounts of food that will keep you fed for up to seven days in remote regions. Make sure you can stay warm in a summer blizzard at high altitude. Bring those waterproof glove protectors and rain booties to keep hands and feet dry and warm.

30. Leave the road and find camp 1.5 to 2.0 hours before dusk. If you happen to get caught in the dark, attach a front LED headlight and rear blinking LED red light. You can carry a blinking strobe light to let traffic know your presence.

Breaking down and packing your bike for travel

Secure the right sized box for your bike. You can buy a plastic box at bike shops if you plan to have a safe place at your destination to store it. If not, a cardboard box will work fine.

Break down your bike by taking off the handlebars, front wheel, pedals, seat and pulling off the rear derailleur. Take the rear derailleur off the dropout, tape it to the chain and encase it in cloth with tape. Do not forget this procedure or you may suffer a bent dropout hanger and possibly a broken rear derailleur. Lock the front forks with a plastic axle and secure it with tape. That will stabilize the forks from breakage. Secure all nuts and bolts and pack the bike with paper so it won't move inside the box. Place the front rack under the forks. The front wheel will fit beside the frame opposite the chain drive side. Tape the pedals to the frame so as not to lose them along with the bike seat and shaft. Slip a piece of cardboard between the wheel and your bike so it won't suffer scratches. Everything you can do to keep the bike locked solidly still in the box is important. Toss in your six-foot fiberglass safety flag and three-foot fiberglass traffic-side safety flag along with empty water bottles. Open the spouts so they won't get disfigured from pressure loss during the flight. Tape the box up with plastic tape. Tape all the four corners, and all seams for extra strength on international journeys where they throw your gear around without regard to damage to your precious bike.

Best safety gear on the planet for cyclists

Let's cover the most important safety device on your bike: be sure to strap that six-foot-long fiberglass pole with orange/lime green and even white safety flag to your rear rack. A second three-foot fiberglass safety pole with orange/lime green flag will fit under your bungee cords that secure your rear pack to the rack—about 18 inches into traffic. In town, you can shove it closer to the bike, so you won't be such a 'wide' profile trying to maneuver around cars in heavy traffic.

The total affect is two orange, flapping flags that can be seen a half-mile away. They get the attention of approaching drivers both front and rear. When you garner their attention, you are less likely to suffer consequences. You must remember that you are sharing the road with at least 2,000 pounds of steel traveling at 65 miles per hour. Just one yawn or sneeze, a glance back at the kids, or a daydream could have a car running up the back of your panniers. Those flags are your lifeline to safety. Engage them as if your life depended on them. Buy at bike shop, K-Mart, Walmart or Target.

Finally, remember you are pedaling down adventure highway. You're an ambassador for your state or country. What you do affects others. Things you say or do last a lifetime to those you encounter. Make your tour a positive experience for all you meet. You will be rewarded with magical moments that last a lifetime in your heart and mind.

CHAPTER 30

Camping techniques, Bear and mountain lion safety, Safe Water, Personal Hygiene, Cooking, Cleaning, Human Waste, Leave No Trace, Wilderness Survival

"To many Americans, the wilderness is little more than a retreat from the tensions of civilization. To others, it is a testing place—a vanishing frontier where humans can rediscover basic values. And to a few, the wilderness is nothing less than an almost holy source of self-renewal. But for every man, woman and child, the ultimate lesson that nature teaches is simply this: man's fate is inextricably linked to that of the world at large, and to all of the other creatures that live upon it." Unknown

Every time you step into the wilderness, it provides you with uncommon splendor and beauty. What can you do to preserve it? Answer: "Leave No Trace!"

By following the established protocol in this chapter whether you ride a bicycle, backpack, climb mountains, fish, raft, canoe, hike, sail or any other wilderness activity—take only photographs and leave only footprints.

For sure, my dad always told me, "Son, when you go camping, always leave the place nicer than you found it."

To this day, I have picked up a half million pieces of trash in my life, if not more. I volunteer to pick up rivers, roadways, campgrounds, mountain paths and any place I see trash. Yes, it's frustrating that many careless outdoor people toss their cans, bottles and glass containers without a blink. I also advocate for a 10-cent deposit/return law like Michigan's to stop the incredible littering of the landscape. It drives me crazy that billions of humans take no responsibility for their landscape around the planet.

Nonetheless, all of us enjoy a stake in our world's well-being and our own as we live this great life adventure. I hope you become one of the people that care and care deeply. This chapter will show you how to preserve the wilderness.

Whether you hike, backpack, canoe, climb, bicycle or any other mode of adventuring—these techniques will guide you.

WILDERNESS CAMPING

CAMPING AND COOKING IN ESTABLISHED CAMPGROUNDS:

Making Camp
Cooking and Food Storage
Camping and Cooking in a Primitive Area
Make Camp in Primitive Areas
Building Campfires Safely in the Wilderness
Fire in Your Tent

Candle Lantern
Sanitation and Human Waste in the Wilderness
Cleaning and Hygiene
Bear and Lion Country
Rules for Camping in Bear and Lion Country
If a Bear or Mountain Lion Should Confront You

When adventuring—shelter and food take on a whole new significance, especially internationally. If you venture into developing countries, being ill-prepared may cause you great discomfort. In the USA, it's not hard to find a camping park, motel, or bed and breakfast. You have many to choose from in every state and most of Canada.

In the developing world outside cities, lodging is next to impossible to find. That's why you must carry your own tent, sleeping bag and air mattress. For cooking meals, you need a stove, cookware, fuel, water and food supplies. When you're prepared with the basics, bicycle adventuring internationally will offer miles of smiles. Nothing beats a good night's sleep on a full stomach.

The most important gear a cyclist can carry is a top-quality tent. It must be big enough, light enough and waterproof. Quick "pitch time" is a nice extra. With so many tents on the market, how do you choose? You may have a friend who knows tents because he/she camps often. They have learned by experience. Have them go to the local camping outfitter with you to discuss the relative differences of tents. Buy good gear. You want to go cheap? Be my guest, but you will pay a terrible price in misery.

If you're on your own, a few tips may help in your purchase. For camping, your tent should be self-standing and six pounds or less. Best bet is a half-dome tent. It should have a waterproof floor and sidewalls. Rip-stop nylon is your best bet for durability, or if you can afford it, buy a Gore-Tex fabric tent. Make sure the tent has a loop to hang clothes and candle lanterns from the ceiling. Make certain the tent is taut enough, so it won't flap in the wind. Get shock-corded poles for easier set up.

Make certain the rain fly covers the outside edges of the tent. Is your tent long enough? Can you sit up in it? Will you have room for two people and your gear? Is it warm enough for three seasons? A light color will be cooler in the summer and stand up under ultraviolet damaging rays better. Zippers should be YKK plastic. Make certain your tent features "No see 'em" netting. Check for good ventilation flow in the tent you buy. Some manufacturers stand solidly behind their tents with excellent guarantees. Compare for a top choice. Purchase seam sealer and apply to the rain fly and corners of the tent, wherever the fabric has been sewn.

Once on the road, a few good habits will keep your tent in top condition for years of use. Purchase a nylon backed plastic tarp for a ground cloth. Cut it to fit 2" inside the outside boundary of your tent. This will help stop sharp objects from cutting your floor and it will keep out moisture. You need to cut it 2" less all around the tent so it won't catch rainwater and pool it in the under you in the middle of the night.

Set up your tent every night as if it was going to rain. Find a high spot in the land and check for rocks and sticks before laying down the tarp. Never leave your tent out in the sun for extended lengths of time. Ultraviolet rays will damage the fabric. When taking down a tent, fold the poles and put them in a safe place immediately after you pull them out of their sleeves. This will prevent them from being stepped on. Count stakes each time you put your tent into the stuff sack. After a rain, either dry out the tent in the morning or at the earliest moment. For storage, make certain your tent is bone dry before putting it away for the winter.

After your tent, purchase a warm, comfortable sleeping bag. You have two choices: goose down or fiber fill. Having used both many times, it's this bicycle camper's opinion that for three season bicycling, a three-pound, 20-degree Fahrenheit, fiber fill mummy bag is your best bet. It dries easier and stands up to usage many years longer. Down shifts and leaves cold spots after a time and the loft breaks down. However, you may have a friend who swears by down for its compactability and lighter weight. It becomes a personal decision.

No matter what your choice, buy a quality mummy bag from a reputable company. Make certain it's long enough and features a contoured hood enclosure with a draw string so all that is not covered when it's cold is your mouth. Make certain your bag is designed so the baffle flap drapes DOWN over the zipper from the inside. Gravity will keep that baffle covering the entire length of the zipper and stop any cold air from entering your bag. Expect to pay more for a down bag. Keep it in a waterproof bag and stuff sack when riding. If you forget, you will be sliding your bare body into a cold, wet bag one night and wonder why you didn't pay attention to these suggestions. Don't laugh, I have slept in wet, cold bags before.

No matter how good your tent and sleeping bag, misery stalks the bicyclist that fails to sleep on an air mattress. The best self-inflating air mattress on the market for cycling is a 3/4 length, 1" thick Thermo-Rest mattress by Cascade Designs. Buy a stuff sack to go with it. It's the best investment for comfort in the world.

While camping you need cookware. A copper-bottomed stainless-steel set with two pots, plastic cups is light and handy. Keep a scrubber and soap in the pot. A plastic fork and spoon are light. If you're traveling in a first world country, go with a propane gas stove, carry two extras. For overseas touring, go with an MSR International stove that burns any kind of fuel. Your Swiss Army knife is a vital part of your cooking utensils, along with a carrot/potato peeler. Add a small plastic cutting board. Always wash cookware after dinner, especially in the wilds. You don't want a grizzly sniffing your toes in the middle of the night.

Depending on how loaded you are, and the length of your adventure, a sleeping bag, tent and mattress will set on your back rack. You may have a front rack with a platform perfect for a sleeping bag. You need a bigger bike to fit this style of packing. Be sure to carry plastic bags to waterproof your sleeping bag. It wouldn't hurt to do the same for your tent and mattress.

The one thing you cannot count on during an adventure is a campground. Well before you begin looking, about 1 1/2 hour before dark, have water bottles filled and an extra full gallon. If the water quality is questionable, purify by tablets, drops or filtration. Purchase your food in advance. Such things as toilet paper, matches and stove fuel should be secured.

If you find a campground with showers and you're willing to pay the price, go for it. Try to keep away from dogs and loud music. Bring along ear plugs to sleep quietly.

Often, you are nowhere near an organized campground, or in the case of developing world, no such thing exists. You're on your own. That's a plus, because it offers you a chance to experience nature, animals and solitude.

The best way to find a campsite is to look for a dirt road that leads into the bush, trees, rocks, or out of sight of the road. If you can find a place near a river, lake or stream, so much the better (Please bathe with biodegradable soap). When you find a suitable spot, away from traffic, pitch your tent, EVERYTIME, as if it were going to rain. Exceptions are the Sahara Desert. I have broken my own rules a few times and it cost me dearly with ruined camera and miserable nights floating around in my tent, or trying to dodge the wet spots creeping up on my body as the bag absorbed more water. Pitch your tent on high ground. Check for rocks, twigs and roots before laying down the ground tarp. Set the front door away from the wind and possible rain. This will give you a wind break for cooking too. Make certain all stakes are secured and the rain fly is taut. Be sure to keep the ground cloth under the tent. Once the tent is secured, take the gear off your bike and put it into your tent. Cable lock your bike to a tree including both wheels. A combination lock will allow everyone in your party to use the same lock without using a key.

CAMPING AND COOKING IN ESTABLISHED CAMPGROUNDS

When camp in an established campground, many obstacles are overcome immediately. You enjoy a picnic table, water, washing facilities and seating area at your command. Nonetheless, you need to buy food and load up on water two to three hours before sunset in case you don't reach and established campground. Always check your map for locations.

Making Camp

After finding a spot in a campground—one to two hours before dark—you can:

31. Pitch your tent on high ground.
32. Roll out the sleeping mattress and sleeping bag.
33. Place all your gear in the tent. Always put your gear in the same places, so you know where to find specific items, even in the dark. Always place your flashlight or miner's lamp exactly in the same place so you can grab it when you need it.
34. Make sure your 'miner's lamp' is on your head and ready to work as darkness falls. These LED headlamps can be purchased at camping outlets. You may look like a coal miner walking around in the dark, but you will find it very useful.
35. Remember NOT to place any food in your tent, especially in bear country. Rule: cook and eat 100 yards from your tent, and then, hang food 100 yards from your tent. That means you may have to eat first, then, cook and eat food, and then, hang food in trees 100 yards from final camp site. Don't believe me? Think you can get away with it? So did I! But when you wake up during the night with a grizzly or black bear pummeling you inside your tent or looking at you when you open the flaps—don't say I didn't warn you! In bear country, always carry bear spray with you from www.REI.com and other camping stores. It could save your life. I guarantee that you will be scared enough to wet your pants, but you could live!
36. If you are not in bear country, you 'can' leave food in your tent as long as you remain in the tent. If you leave, or you have food odor in your tent, little critters will eat their way through the nylon and ruin your tent.
37. Lock your bike to a tree or to your helmet inside your tent (if there are no trees or something to cable the bike). To do this, run the cable through the bike frame, then into your tent and lock it to your helmet strap. When you zip up the tent, the cable acts like an umbilical cord between it and your bike. If someone tries to make

off with your bike, they won't get far before you notice half your tent being pulled away.

38. Always light the match before turning on your gas burner. Never turn the gas on first, unless you want to make like a Saturn rocket and blast yourself to the moon.

39. Set up your food and fixings, cutting board, utensils, pans, water bottles and spices.

40. Prepare your meal.

41. Enjoy!

42. Wash, clean, dry all your pots and utensils. Replace and secure.

43. Secure food in tree or bear box, or if you're looking for an exciting night of terror, leave it in your tent!

Cooking and Food Storage

Before cooking your meal, make good use of the stove burner for heating water for tea or hot chocolate. If you're cooking by a campfire, let the wood burn down so you get an even heat from the coals. You'll also have to tackle the problem of balancing pots on the coals.

Once you have prepared the food for cooking by chopping and cutting, place the food into the cooking pot. As your dinner progresses, keep any eye on the food to keep it from burning.

After dinner, wash everything with soap and rinse with water. Leave no food out for the animals. Keep extra food in a locked food box—a wooden or metal box used in some campgrounds where animals are a concern. If there are no food boxes, and you're in bear or mountain lion country, do not store food in your tent. Hang your food in a tree 300 feet from your camp.

Leave none of your gear out in the rain. Either store it in the tent or under the tent vestibule.

Camping and Cooking in a Primitive Area

Camping in primitive (wilderness) areas presents several challenges that must be considered. You must be more responsible to your environment, i.e., disposal of human waste, water contamination and generated food and paper waste. You are more susceptible to bears, raccoons, squirrels and wild pigs charging into your camp looking for food. If it's a big old grizzly, he might be looking for you because he carries the latest copy of the **Gourmet Bear in Search of a Bicyclist.** Take precautions when camping in the wilds.

Again, make certain you have loaded up on extra water two to three hours before dusk. Or carry a filter that can purify water if there are ample places to fetch it—such as in the mountains or in lake regions.

Next, look for a campsite well off the road and hidden away from the sight of others. Not only is it a good idea to 'vanish' into the wilderness for personal safety, you will sleep better without hearing traffic all night. Remember your earplugs and use them!

Most dirt roads or trails on public land will lead to a 'stealth' camping spot. Try to get behind trees, brush, hills or a mountain. You want to be concealed, along with your fire or candlelight.

Be certain to keep your tent 25 feet away from fire. Ashes will burn through the nylon in seconds. Place your tent on high ground, so that if it rains, you won't wake up feeling like you're being swept over Niagara Falls. Special note: eight out of ten persons reading this advice will choose to learn this lesson the hard way! Trust me, you will wake up in the middle of the night wishing you sported gills!

Make Camp in Primitive Areas

44. Secure food and 1.5 gallons of water two or three hours before dusk.
45. Look for an abandoned road or trail and 'vanish' into the landscape.
46. Pitch your tent on high ground. The sight should be safe from lightning and potential washout from a rainstorm.
47. Roll out your air mattress and sleeping bag.

48. Place all your gear in exact same place every night.
49. Place your miner's lamp near your headrest. Once your tent and gear are secured inside, either lock your bike to a tree or run the cable from the bike to your helmet inside your tent.
50. If you have a campfire, make sure it is 25 feet away from your tent. If that is not possible, use your stove for cooking.
51. Spread your tablecloth on the ground outside your tent. Tablecloth can be a yard square of plastic.
52. Secure your candle lantern where you can use it.
53. Organize all your cooking gear and food in front of you.
54. If you are using a stove, make sure it's stable. You don't need a scalding injury while away from medical help.
55. If you drink coffee, hot chocolate or tea, boil your water first.
56. Prepare food. Cook food. Eat like a ravenous wild maniac that you are!
57. Wash dishes and clean up all traces of food.
58. Always leave the bottom zipper of your tent open if you leave camp to take a bath or for any other reason. Whether you have food in the tent or not, curious squirrels or chip monks may bite their way through the nylon to see what's inside.

Building Campfires Safely in the Wilderness

If you enjoy ashes in your soup and burning embers in your potatoes, make yourself happy—cook on an open fire! It's SO romantic and mountain-manish! It's primordial! Humans have enjoyed campfires before the wheel they invented the wheel. It beats watching television, unless you think watching the latest episode of "American Idol" gives meaning to life.

You need to remember a few points about making a fire to keep it safe and under control:

59. Always check for, and obey, no-burn rules. Use common sense when camping in a dry area.

60. Build a protective rock ring around the fire. You can wet the ground around the fire ring if you have ample water.

61. Keep the fire away from tents and other fabrics. Watch out for your Lycra or Gore-Tex. One flying ember will burn a hole in it.

62. Keep your eyes on the fire at all times.

63. Build the fire away from overhanging tree branches or dry brush. If you build under some low-hanging branches, you might turn the tree into a bonfire. Explain that to the local fire department chief after you've taken her away from her husband and two kids at supper-time. On second thought, maybe she would mind a little adventure away from hubby and the kids...! Finally, avoid building a fire against a large rock or cliff because it will leave unsightly smoke scars.

64. Keep a water supply handy in case you need to douse the flames.

65. Let the fire burn down before you place your pots in the embers. You want a slow, even heat on your food.

66. If it's windy, eat pork and beans out of a can, or a sandwich, or energy bars. Avoid the chance of a runaway fire.

67. Before hitting the sack, be certain to put the fire COMPLETELY OUT by smothering it with water or dirt. If you fail to put it out completely, you could cost people their lives and homes. Put that fire out COMPLETELY!

68. When finished with the fireplace, spread the rocks out and return the fire area to its natural appearance. Spread the ashes and place leaves and brush over the fire pit. Really give nature a chance by keeping the wild beautiful. "Leave no trace!"

Fire in Your Tent

On those rainy or windy days, your first inclination might be to cook in your tent. Don't!

Okay, I know you're starving to death and you hunger for a Big Mac, or Chipotle's Special or a Giant pizza. Again, don't cook in your tent!

There are so many little things that can and will go wrong when you have an open flame burning in your tent. I'm as careful as a person can be, but once, I nearly turned my tent into a bonfire! Avoid learning this lesson the hard way.

Candle Lantern

The only flame, and I haven't done it in a long time because of miner's lamps with LEDs, is a glass and aluminum-encased candle lantern. Even then, I never leave it in the tent unattended. Make sure it's either hanging from the roof on a string, or resting on a flat surface such as a notepad or book.

Fire inside your tent is nothing to fool with, and that's not a lesson you want to learn the hard way!

Sanitation and Human Waste in the Wilderness

It's very important to follow a few rules when camping in primitive wilderness situations:

When washing dishes, heat the water and use bio-degradable soap. If you're washing in a lake or stream, make sure you discard the soapy water onto the soil at least 15 feet away from the lake or stream water so it drains into the soil. Rinse your cooking gear thoroughly.

Pack out what you pack in! I pick up trash of careless campers. I honor Mother Nature by leaving a place cleaner than I found it. In the immortal words of the great philosopher Goethe, "Do not think that you can do so little, that you do nothing at all." Avoid burning anything, especially plastic, but do take it in a bag to a proper trash can up in the next town or wherever it's proper and responsible.

Since no toilets are available in primitive campsites, please follow strict wilderness rules:

69. Find a spot 20 to 30 yards away from your campsite and away from a water source.

70. Dig a hole four to six inches deep. Do your business. Cover your waste with soil. If that is not possible, cover with a rock or leaves. Carry your TP in a 1-gallon zip lock plastic bag and another 1-gallon zip lock bag inside it. Roll your 'soiled' TP into a ball with new TP and place it in the second zip lock bag. No, you don't have to touch the soiled TP. Again, "Leave No Trace!"

71. You may burn your used toilet paper in the campfire. If dry conditions exist or combustibles are present, just carry the used TP in the zip lock bag and toss used TP at the next proper disposal.

72. In Chile, my friend Doug nearly burned an entire wheat field because the flame he used to burn his toilet paper ignited to the dry stalks. The next thing I knew, Doug waddled toward me with his shorts around his knees, screaming, "I just crapped in the wrong place!" We grabbed six water bottles and ran back to the fire, squirting it with our tiny water guns. A passing motorist and an old lady stopped to help us. You can imagine her shock and confusion when she saw Doug with his shorts at his ankles and me screaming and squirting at the flames. She didn't know whether to help us or faint. Moral of this episode: be careful where you strike a match to your toilet paper—and pull up your pants before you light it!

73. Also, clean your hands with 'hand sanitization' or soap and water, or at least rinse your hands.

74. One last point: if you've used up your toilet paper, you will be forced to use your fingers to wipe your butt. Simply take your water bottle, pour some water into your hand, and then, wash your butt. Repeat until your butt is clean of all fecal matter.

75. After you're clean around your butt, you must wash your hands with soap and water to make sure you've got clean fingers and hand. If you've run out of soap, you must rinse your fingers until you feel you've cleaned them the best you could possibly clean them.

Cleaning and Hygiene

While on tour or any adventure, you're living at a basic level. You're closer to being an animal than you've ever been. Bugs will try to invade your tent and mosquitos will buzz around your head. Spiders will spin webs across your tent at night and they will be eating their 'catch' when you step out the next day. You'll go to sleep under moonlight and wake up with the sun. The morning alarm clock might be the laughing call of an Australian kookaburra bird. It's natural, but it's dirty out there on a bike, or backpacking, or mountain climbing or any extended outdoor activity.

That's why you must maintain good sanitation and hygiene practices. Wash your hands before preparing food. Be certain to use bio-degradable soap in the wilderness. If you don't have any, use any soap or hand cleaner, but make sure you use it. Avoid throwing soapy water into a stream or lake. Throw it onto the land where it can drain into the soil.

After any use of pots and pans, make certain to wash and rinse them. Use your camp towel to wipe them or let them dry in the sun. Please honor Mother Nature and she will bless you with wonders around the next bend in the road or turn of the river.

Bear and Lion Country

"Bears are made of the same dust as we, and breathe the same winds and drink of the same waters. A bear's days are warmed by the same sun, his dwellings are overdomed by the same blue sky, and his life turns and ebbs with the heart pulsing like ours. He was poured from the same fountain. And whether he at last goes to our stingy Heaven or not, he has terrestrial immortality. His life, not long, not short, knows no beginning, no ending. To him life unstinted, unplanned, is above accidents of time, and his years, markless and boundless, equal eternity," John Muir, hiking in Yosemite Valley, California, 1839

Camping in Grizzly, Black Bear and Mountain Lion Country

The grizzly is North America's symbol of wilderness. His domain reaches from Yellowstone to Alaska. To catch a glimpse of this great animals fills your eyes with wonder. His wildness defines the wilderness. He remains "king" in his domain.

Nothing will scare the daylights out of you faster than coming face to face with a bear. Few animals will kill you faster than a grizzly if she feels threatened. If she comes in the night, you will feel terror like never before because you have the added uncertainty of darkness. The sound of her grunting will drive your heart into a pumping frenzy, and your blood will race around your body like a Formula One race car at the Indy 500.

I shivered in my sleeping bag while a grizzly dragged his muzzle across the side of my tent one morning in Alaska. His saliva left a mark on the nylon for a few weeks, and a mark for a lifetime on my mind. I'll never forget the three-and-a-half-inch claws that tore through the back of my tent…that day. I lucked out!

Bears prove capricious, unpredictable and dangerous. They search for food 24/7. Anything that looks edible to them makes for fair game. They eat berries, salmon, moose, deer, mice and humans without discrimination.

That's why this section deals with camping in grizzly bear, black bear and mountain lion country.

If you travel, hike and camp in remote regions of North America, or other areas of the world, sooner or later, you will camp in bear country. It's not something to be feared, but it is something you must respect. You travel through his dining room.

The key to your safety and survival in Mr. Grizzly's domain: respect! You must honor the rules of the wilderness. You must follow those rules each and every time you camp, hike or otherwise make your way into his territory. You may not get a second chance.

Imagine looking into a grizzly's eyes, backed by his 800 pounds of teeth and claws, and pleading, "Gee, Mr. Bear, could you give me a break this time…I'm really story I left my chocolate chip cookies inside my tent…can we make a deal, like, I'll give you my first-born child… please, pretty please…."

Never assume a bear won't walk into your life.

At the same time, you cannot camp in fear. During my many journeys to Alaska, I enjoyed extraordinary moments watching rogue grizzlies fishing for salmon and mother grizzlies playing with their cubs. Great wonder and amazing moments!

I also had the living hell scared out of me because of my own carelessness.

By using common sense and following the rules, you can minimize the chances and danger of a bear confrontation. But your safety cannot be guaranteed. You could do everything right, and still run into a bear—especially if he's trying to find food for his evening dinner.

However, since I've alarmed you, let me put this in proper perspective. Former Governor Sarah Palin lives in Alaska, and she alleges she has outrun a few grizzly bears. Therefore, if you're camping with Sarah, the only thing you have to do: run faster than her!

If you follow nature's rules, your chances of a bear confrontation are less than a lightning strike. Therefore, go ahead and enjoy yourself. And if you do encounter a bear, you will return home with great bear stories that will keep your friends glued to your every word.

Remember: food and food odors attract bears, which makes them overcome their fear of humans. Be smart and keep food odor off your body and ten, and away from your camping site.

Rules for Camping in Bear Country

Camp in an area least likely to be visited by bears. Stay away from animal trails, large droppings, diggings, berry bushes, beehives and watering holes. Don't swim in streams where salmon run. If you do, you may end up running for your own life.

Make absolutely certain your tent has no food odor in or on it. If you have spilled jam or peanut butter, grizzlies especially like Skippy's Crunch Style, on your tent fabric, wash it clean.

Cook 300 feet away from your tent. Wash your gear thoroughly. Do not sleep in the same clothes that you wore while eating and cooking dinner.

Make sure you avoid keeping perfume, deodorant or toothpaste in your tent. Keep anything that has an odor in your food bag and hang it away from your camp.

Hang your food in a strong 3.1-millimeter-thick plastic bag at least 300 feet from your tent. That means your camp, cooking and food hanging areas are in a triangle, 300 feet apart. If a bear does amble into your sector, he will go after your food bag, and more than likely, he won't bother you.

Bear-proof canisters that can carry several days of food supplies cost about $100.00 and can be purchased at most camping outlets mentioned in this book. www.REI.com

After you have hung your food, take out a wet cloth and wipe your face and hands to ensure you have no food odor on them.

Finally, brush and floss your teeth. You wouldn't want a tiny piece of food between your molars to be the reason you inadvertently invited Mr. Grizz to feast upon your tenderloin body at night. Can you imagine the coroner's report in Whitehorse, Yukon, "A grizzly bear mauled a gourmet camper last night because he left one little piece of fried chicken between his teeth...he could have starred in the movie "Dumb and Dumber.""

Also, remember to employ the same sanitation rules you learned in the primitive camping section.

Hanging food: Attach one end of a parachute cord to a rock or carabineer and throw it over a tree limb. Use the other end of the cord to tie your food bag. Pull the bag into the air at least 12 feet above the ground, at least five feet from the tree trunk and at least five feet from the limb where the cord is hanging. Secure the parachute cord by tying it to a limb at the base of the tree or some other tree.

A second method for hanging food: Loop two bags over a limb so they balance each other and let them dangle with no tie-off cord. Some bears have figured out to follow the tie-off cord and release it by batting or pawing it—mostly in Yellowstone where so many careless campers visit. This second method should discourage a bear's efforts. Again, keep it 12 feet off the round, at least five feet away from tree trunk.

A third method: throw a line over the branches of two trees about ten feet apart. Throw the same parachute cord over the line and hang your food bag between the trees on the line. Do what works best for you.

Grizzlies do not intentionally prey on humans. As long as they are not drawn to any food odor, you should enjoy a good night's sleep.

If a Bear or Mountain Lion Should Confront You

Okay, you've followed the rules, but you wake up to the sounds of a bear outside your tent, or something else that's breathing and prowling through the night mist. Your nostrils fill with the stench of something that's got a really bad case of body odor.

You don't carry a gun, but you do have your Swiss Army knife! Yeah, great! The bear would snatch it out of your hands and use it for a toothpick afterwards! If you did carry a gun, it would only piss him off! But you kept your bear repellant spray right next to your sleeping bag, so you pull it out. Yes, bear spray will stop a grizzly better than a gun.

At that moment, you wish you could sprint like an NFL halfback or fly like an eagle!

What to do: Stay calm. Remember that bears and mountain lions don't like humans. It could be a deer, moose or elk. Unless you're in bear country in early spring, when a bear is just out of his den and hungry, he may only be curious and sniffing around.

I have been told that a good strategy is to play dead inside your sleeping bag if you're attacked by a grizzly. If you're with another person, you may opt to run in different directions. At least one of you would live! Keep that bear spray in your hand! Personally, I carry two bottles of bear spray. No hard and fast rules exist that guarantee anything in this situation.

During the day, be alert. If you come in contact with a grizzly, try to move out his area. Never run! Make a lot of noise by blowing on a whistle if you're hiking. If a bear sees you and charges, turn sideways and do not look at him directly, but do point your bear spray at his face. He may still attack you, but then again, if you are not threatening, he may not. If he continues charging to within 15 to 20 feet, spray a stream of bear spray at his nose, and follow the stream with your own eyes until you hit him right on the nose and continue the stream. It will stop him. Make sure your friend carries a second can of spray to continue the point-blank spraying if needed. Some folks carry wasp & hornet spray for backup.

If you don't have bear spray, shame on you, but if the attack continues, drop to the ground and assume the cannonball position with your hands over your head to protect your head and stomach.

If you run, he mostly like will chase you down. At this juncture, you may want to...cry, pray, scream or faint. It may not do any good, but it may make you feel better. If your prayer isn't working, make a quick conversion to another religion and pray faster. If you die, you died while on a great adventure, which makes it a bit heroic. It's better to die this way rather than suffering a heart attacks while eating chocolate bon bons on a Barker Lounger in front of an NFL game with the remote glued to your hand.

Black bears: when confronting black bears, you have a much better chance of survival. Stand your ground. Do not drop to the ground or play dead. Don't look into his eyes; stay on your feet and keep that bear spray pointed right at his nose. Don't look scared, even if you're wetting your pants with fear. Maintain your composure until the black bear leaves your area. Practice using the bear spray or hornet spray.

Mountain lion: if confronted with a mountain lion or puma, stand your ground and make yourself appear larger if possible by spreading out your hands and/or hopping up on a log or rock. Move away slowly and keep the 'bear' spray aimed at the lion. If you have a child with you, pick him or her up and hold the child close to you. With a cat, you can fight back, and it may run away. It also may run if you throw rocks at it. Do not run yourself. Again, it's between you and lady luck.

Adventure is not always comfortable, but it is still adventure. I am a firm believer that neither bliss or adventure are ever obtained by staying home in your rocking chair.

As a final note, be confident that you will make your way through bear country safely when you follow the rules of Mother Nature. When you respect Mother Nature, she will respect you right back.

I can see you sitting around the table with your friends after your adventure in Alaska:

In your journal, "Yeah, I woke up one morning on the Kenai River when I heard a blood-curdling growl…I thought the sun was shining through my mosquito netting, but it was the pearly whites of a thousand pound grizzly…well sir, I didn't have much time to think, so I pulled out my Bowie Knife—kinda' like Daniel Boone—and stared back into that grizzly's eyes. That's when I gave him a toothy growl of my own. It scared him so badly, he scrambled up a tree, where we used him for an umbrella to keep the 24-hour sun from burning down on us while we ate fresh salmon steaks on the campfire and talked to Alaska Governor Sarah Palin in the next campsite."

Jack London would have been proud!

Tent Camping

Release the valve on the air mattress first so it is ready when you get everything inside. A key to camping success is having everything where you want it, when you need it. That means replacing the same gear in the same pouch every single time you use it. ALWAYS zip up a pouch immediately after taking out or putting something into it. Make it a habit.

Before cooking dinner, you might want to take a bath first, before the sun goes down and the air cools. Soap, towel and shower shoes are all you need. If it's a swiftly moving stream, be careful with your bottle of biodegradable soap.

A special note on campfires. Gather your wood before dark. Pick up kindling and larger branches. Stick with dead wood. Be sure the fire pit is a safe distance from your tent. Sparks carry on the breeze and will melt nylon in seconds. Make certain the flames won't catch adjoining grass or overhanging branches on fire. A circular rock firewall is a good safety factor. Place paper and kindling at the bottom. Light the fire, get it going and keep adding larger and larger wood until you have a good flame. If you cook on and open fire, keep your pot in a heavy plastic bag to keep the black soot from smudging your gear. If your campsite is in a dry zone where fire hazards are high, use common sense when building a fire, and decide not to build one, if it's a high wind area. ALWAYS put the fire totally out with water at night and in the morning. Clean the pit and spread the rocks around. Replace twigs and leaves over the pit before you leave.

When you're ready for sleep, use one of your panniers for a pillow and a sweater to make a cushion. Or, purchase an air pillow at a camping store. Be certain to check for mosquitos by shining your flashlight around the tent. If you see one, kill the devil. Now you're ready for sleep. Or are you? If you are in deep wilderness where bears or other large meat-eating animals live, leave no food in your tent. Put it in a plastic bag and hang it in a tree, 300 feet from your tent. Be certain to brush your teeth, and wash your face and hands so no food odor is on your person. If you have fruit in your tent, and it's touching the floor, ants will cut the nylon in a few hours. Don't give them the chance. Any time you leave camp for a hike, do not leave food in the tent, and leave it open so chipmunks can get in. If they can't, they will chew holes through your tent.

In the morning, you may need to take your daily constitutional. That's fine. Just remember the rules of camping. Bury your feces if possible. As for your toilet paper, burn it, bury it or wrap it up and carry it out to throw away or burn at an appropriate time. When burning it, use prudent judgment in high fire areas of dry grass. It's that simple. In fact, leave the campsite cleaner than you found it. Burn or carry out the trash and put in a proper disposal. No matter how trashed a place is, you don't have to become a part of the problem, you can be a part of the solution.

When breaking camp, pack your gear and clean out the tent. Pull your stakes and count them before dropping in the bag. Do not let them lay on the ground where they can get stepped on. Fold the tent along with ground cloth and place in the stuff sack. You might try changing your folding pattern periodically, so you don't cause premature deterioration on waterproofing and fabric. Strap your gear on the bike. Walk the bike out of the area, and go back to look over everything to see that you have all your gear, including the food bag that hung from the tree. Don't be surprised if you walk up on a bear scratching his head trying to figure out how to get to your food bag.

When you're satisfied that you have everything secured, it's time to pedal. If the camp site was beautiful, you may have taken a few photographs for memories of your home in the woods.

When you follow a solid routine for camping each night, you wake up refreshed and relaxed. Camping goes hand in hand for great wilderness adventures.

"A blank spot on the map dances with your imagination. What treasures might it hold? As you swing your leg over the top tube, your touring bike allows you unlimited freedom of flight for your body, mind and spirit. Slip your hands into your riding gloves. Grab those handlebars. Press your feet onto the pedals. Click the brake handles. Slide your rear-end onto the saddle. Look toward the distant horizon that beckons your dreams. Feel the energy coursing through your body. Make that first pedal stroke downward as your thighs lift you onto adventure highway. Time means nothing now. It slips away as easily as grains of sand on a wind-swept beach. But those grains only trade places. On your bike, you move into that blank spot—new locations in the passage of time. The pedaling becomes incidental—like breathing. The hills and mountains come

and go—your legs powering over them in a kind of winsome trance. Grappling with headwinds brings determination; while riding a tailwind fetches ecstasy. You transform into a state of bliss, much like an eagle gliding over majestic mountains. You see them soaring, just living. You soar with them as you glide down a mountain grade. Those moments present you with uncommon experiences that give your life eternal expectation. That's bicycle adventure!" FHW

CHAPTER 31

Important References
for Bicycle Touring

"An ounce of knowledge prevents a boat-load of learning it the hard way." FHW

After reading this bicycle adventure book, you might want to dip your toes into the "Bicycle Touring World." For certain, tens of thousands of men and women worldwide travel via bicycle. They sling their panniers over the racks and take off for weekends, week long tours, a month and even three months. Others save their money to launch themselves into one, two and three year bicycle trips around the world. Retirees fulfill their dreams by bicycle touring around the planet.

While you might have enjoyed the journey via the written word and a few pictures, to ride in the saddle, crank those pedals and play the game yourself, proves infinitely more fun for your body, mind and spirit. It's a kind of magic that I tried to capture in words at the front-end of each chapter, and if I did, great! I hope you're moved to create your own exploration of this wondrous planet. This last chapter shows you how to connect.

From Chapters 29 and 30, you possess all the information you need to move you into the bicycle touring arena. Take it a little bite at a time. Get your feet wet before diving into it full bore.

For certain, you need to get into physical condition. It's true, you could start out being a bit overweight, but not much. Why? If you're 40 to 50 or more pounds overweight, riding on a bicycle seat day after day will kill your butt bones and turn your butt muscles into pain points. While the Aero bars will ease the weight off your rear-end, in the end, you must start out in lean condition. Or, you might possess the tenacity to endure your butt pain until you pedal your calories away and lose weight. I've seen men and women lose 50 to 80 pounds while on tour. If they can do it, you can do it.

If you want this adventure badly enough, you can join health clubs, engage personal trainers, weight loss programs and the like to move your body to where it can enjoy the rigors of bicycle travel. There are plenty of programs, so find the one that fits you.

To give you a little background and proof that you can succeed, I met my old college roommate 40 years later by accident. He moved to Colorado after retiring. When we parted ways in college, he enjoyed 6'1" and 180 pounds. When I saw him again a lifetime later, he walked into the restaurant at 6'1" and 280 pounds. To say the least, I could see he wouldn't live very long in his retirement. He faced a heart attack at 55 years of age. Sad, because he enjoyed unlimited wealth.

Since I plan my bicycle adventures two years in advance, I told him of my forthcoming trip to bicycle from Nord Kapp, Norway on the Arctic Ocean, to Athens, Greece, he enthusiastically said, "Man, that sounds incredible…can I ride with you and your buddies?"

I said, "Bob, you're so obese, you would die of a heart attack on the first climb up a mountain, and/or, your ass would cause you so much pain within two days, that you couldn't walk, let alone pedal a bike."

"What if I lost it?" he asked.

"If you get back down to 180 pounds and take a stress test," I said. "I'll take you. But be-forewarned. This will be in the maritime of

Norway in June with cold winds and rains. My other buddies are hard core. No pissing, moaning, carping, bitching or complaining. If you want this adventure badly enough, you must understand its parameters. Above all, you must steel yourself with "true grit" to attempt such a monumental journey."

"You got it," he said.

At the bon voyage party two years later, he walked into the room at 185 pounds. I about fell out of my chair.

"I'm ready," he said, showing me his stress test results.

His wife said, "Thank you for saving Bob's life."

Today, he enjoys incredible memories and pictures from that European adventure. But he didn't stop with that one lone trip. He rides the finest touring bike with top-notch panniers and gear. He succeeded in riding coast-to-coast across America with me. He loves to pedal and he loves touring. At nearly 75, he's got passion, purpose and energy in his life. He's ridden the West Coast and Ragbrai. All because of bicycle touring. Oh, and he stopped smoking and drinking. I'm so proud of him for transforming his life. So are his kids and grandkids, plus his wife.

If Bob could do it, I swear that you can do it.

To get your feet wet, you can buy this magazine and go to Facebook for bicycle touring pages. The magazine shows you everything you need to know about touring all over the world. The social media pages give you stories and advice of every kind.

Adventure Bicycling Magazine offers you the best in every category of bicycle touring. www.AdventureCycling.org

Additionally, they feature "Companions Wanted" where you can hook up with anyone wanting a partner for a specific ride. Some ask for a week, women only, men only, gays only and other specifications. You write your own advertisement. The magazine features stories from others who have traveled through specific tours globally. By joining, you will become a member along with 60,000 other cyclists.

They also feature guided tours for a week, month, coast-to-coast, Alaska and more.

In the United States, you may pedal the Southern Tier, Central Tier and Northern Tier coast-to-coast routes marked on Adventure Cycling maps. You may enjoy the fabulous West Coast Tour, Continental Divide Tour, Lewis & Clark Trail Tour, Katy Trail, East Coast Tour from Maine to Key West, Florida, Erie Canal Tour, Rails to Trails Tours, The Mitt of Michigan, circumnavigation of the lower 48 states and dozens more. The maps detail elevation, camping spots, food stores and scenic locations along the route.

You might enjoy a coast-to-coast across Canada. From Vancouver, British Columbia to Newfoundland and Labrador. Say high to my long-distance touring friend in St. Foy, Quebec, since 1981: Monsieur Denis LeMay. We have pedaled the Continental Divide, Southern Tier Tour and all of Europe.

In the rear of the magazine, you will find touring companies from America, Mexico, South America, Europe, Asia, Africa, Australia and more.

You may find bicycle touring groups from every age.

Also, you may want to become a member of www.warmshowers. org : They feature 117,000 members with 71,000 hosts in 17 countries, who host touring cyclists for a night or two for the cost of fellowship. The hosts love cyclists from around the world.

On Facebook, you may join dozens of cyclists at:

All things Bicycling and Bikes
Cycling Fun
Biking Quotes
Bicycle Touring & Bikepacking
Expedition Bicycle nomads
Bicycle touring (rider's forum)
Bicycle Writers: Tales of the road
Rails to Trails
Bicycle Touring Stories
Long Distance Cycling
Touring on a Bicycle

Endurance ride and bikepacking
The Path Less Traveled
Solo Male and Female touring cyclists
Cycling Past Fifty
Cycling over 60
Cycling 65 – 100 +
Viva la Bicycleta
Adventure Cycling Association
Cycling Lifestyle
Bicycle Culture
Bicycle Touring North America
Bicycle Touring Explorers (forum)
Bicycle Touring UK and Mainland Europe
Cycling Canada
Cycling Australia
Safe Cycling Australia

That will get you started. May you live on the "edge of wonder" on all your bicycle adventures.

The End

About the Author

Frosty Wooldridge lives each day with boundless enthusiasm, gratitude and a sense of purpose for everything he undertakes. He graduated from Michigan State University. He loves mountain climbing, scuba diving, swing dancing, skiing and bicycle touring. He writes and speaks on overpopulation and environmental challenges facing humanity. He has taught at the elementary, high school and college levels. He has rafted, canoed, backpacked, sailed, windsurfed, snowboarded and more all over the planet. He has bicycled 100,000 miles on six continents and 14 times across the United States. His feature articles have appeared in national and international magazines for 30 years. He has interviewed on NBC, CBS, ABC, CNN, FOX and 100 radio shows. He presents a motivational program with a dramatic worldwide travel slide show to church groups, high schools, colleges, civic clubs and other organizations: **How to Live a Life of Adventure: Designing Your Own Life on Your Own Terms**. His website contains more information for anyone aspiring toward a spectacular life:

www.HowtoLiveaLifeofAdventure.com

Facebook adventure pages:

How to Live a Life of Adventure: The Art of Exploring the World

Bicycle Touring Unique Moments

Bicycling Poets

Acknowledgements

Special thanks to Dr. Cynthia Schoen for brilliant copy editing along with ideas for creating a compelling and motivational piece of literature. Thanks to my fabulous wife Sandi for her treasured ideas and daily support. Extraordinary thanks goes to my college roommate and best friend Bob Johannes who brought scholarly ideas, wisdom and constructive criticism to this book. Thank each of you from my heart to yours. Additionally, thank you Frank Cauthorn, Don Lindahl, Bob Johannes and Dave Turner for your incredible essays on what it means to be a long-distance touring cyclist.

Book cover: Left to right—Frosty Wooldridge, Robert Case, Gerry Mulroy and Don Lindahl.

OTHER BOOKS BY THE AUTHOR

Handbook for Touring Bicyclists—Bicycling touring grows in popularity each year. Men and women around the world take to the highways and the "open air" is their kitchen. On the pages of this book, you'll discover how to buy, carry, prepare and store food while on tour. Discover the ins and outs with a "Baker's Dozen" of touring tips that are essential for successful bicycle adventuring. Whether you're going on a weekend ride, a weeklong tour or two years around the world, this handbook will help you learn the artistry of bicycling and cooking.

Strike Three! Take Your Base—The Brookfield Reader, Sterling, VA. To order this hardcover book, send $19.95 to Frosty Wooldridge by contacting him through his website. This poignant story is important reading for every teen who has ever experienced the loss of a parent from either death or divorce. This is the story of a boy losing his father and growing through his sense of pain and loss. It is the story of baseball, a game that was shared by both the boy and his father, and how baseball is much like life.

An Extreme Encounter: Antarctica— "This book transports readers into the bowels of million-year-old glaciers, katabatic winds, to the tops of smoking volcanoes, scuba diving under the ice, intriguing people, death, outlaw activities and rare moments where the author meets penguins, whales, seals and Skua birds. Hang on to your seat belts.

You're in for a wild ride where the bolt goes into the bottom of the world." Sandy Colhoun, editor-in-chief, The Antarctic Sun

Bicycling Around the World: Tire Tracks for your Imagination— "This book mesmerizes readers with animal stories that bring a smile to your face. It chills you with a once-in-a-lifetime ride in Antarctica where you'll meet a family of Emperor penguins. Along the way, you'll find out that you have to go without a mirror, sometimes, in order to see yourself. The greatest aspect of this book comes from—expectation. Not since *Miles from Nowhere* has a writer captured the Zen and Art of Bicycle Adventure as well as Wooldridge. Not only that, you may enjoy a final section: "Everything you need to know about long distance touring." He shows you "How to live the dream." You will possess the right bike, equipment, money and tools to ride into your own long-distance touring adventures. If you like bicycling, you'll go wild reading this book. If you don't like bicycling, you'll still go wild reading this book." Jon Sutton

Motorcycle Adventure to Alaska: Into the Wind— "Seldom does a book capture the fantasy and reality of an epic journey the magnitude of this book. Trevor and Dan resemble another duo rich in America's history of youthful explorers who get into all kinds of trouble—Tom Sawyer and Huckleberry Finn. They plied the Mississippi River, but Dan and his brother push their machines into a wild and savage land—Alaska. My boys loved it." John Mathews, father of two boys and a daughter.

Bicycling the Continental Divide: Slice of Heaven, Taste of Hell— "This bicycle dream ride carries a bit of mountain man adventure. The author mixes hope with frustration, pain with courage and bicycling over the mountains. John Brown, a friend left behind to battle cancer, provides guts and heart for his two friends who ride into the teeth of nature's fury. Along the way, you'll laugh, cry and gain new appreciations while pondering the meaning of life." Paul Jackson

Losing Your Best Friend: Vacancies of the Heart— "This is one heck of a powerful book. It's a must read for anyone that has lost a friend or parent. It will give you answers that you may not have thought about. It will touch your heart and you will learn from their experiences. It also shows you what you can do if you suffer conflict with your friend's wife or girlfriend." Jonathan Runy

Rafting the Rolling Thunder— "Fasten your raft-belts folks. You're in for the white-water rafting ride of your life. Wooldridge keeps readers on the edge of their seats on a wild excursion through the Grand Canyon. Along the way, he offers you an outlaw-run by intrepid legend "High Water Harry," a man who makes a bet with the devil and nearly loses his life. The raft bucks beneath you as Harry crashes through Class V rapids. And the Grand Canyon Dish Fairies, well, they take you on separate rides of laughter and miles of smiles. Enjoy this untamed excursion on a river through time." Jason Rogers

How to Deal with 21st Century American Women: Co-Creating a Successful Relationship— "The chapters on the nine key points for creating a successful long-term relationship are the best suggestions for anyone considering marriage. Every woman should read them along with her man. This is the first male relationship book that honors the male perspective and aims for sensible collaboration. I highly recommend this book for men and women." Chelsea Robinson

How to Live a Life of Adventure: The Art of Exploring the World— "If you endeavor to live like you mean it, to aspire to show up with passion and purpose, and take your being to maximum heart rate in mind and body—please allow Frosty to coach, inspire and guide you. *How to Live a Life of Adventure* will rock your body and soul, and enliven within you your belief and practice of living like you mean it— with passion and purpose." Dr. James Rouse, world traveler, Founder of Optimum Wellness Media.

America on the Brink: The Next Added 100 Million Americans— "Electrifying reading! This is a veritable cannonade of a book. Wooldridge targets the people and institutions, from the president of the USA on down, who refuse to look at the consequences of population growth in the modern era. His focus is on the United States, but his range is the world. He fearlessly addresses issues that politicians fear to mention, such as the effects of mass immigration on our population future and social systems. He engages leaders to force population issues into our local and national political decisions." Lindsey Grant, former Deputy Assistant Secretary of State for Environment and Population.

Living Your Spectacular Life— "This book entertains, inspires and motivates. What I liked most about it: Wooldridge offers other motivational writers in each chapter to give you new ideas on living a spectacular life. He wants you to succeed for your sake. If that means you enjoy a greater affinity to another writer, he gives you plenty of choices. He's got six concepts and six practices that provide you with personal courage, self-confidence and empowerment. He offers you dozens of ordinary men and women living spectacular lives in various pursuits from world travel to growing a garden. He kept me reading through every chapter." Jake Hodges

All books available at: 1 888 280 7715, www.amazon.com, www. barnesandnoble.com, also on Kindle.

PRAISE FOR: OLD MEN
BICYCLING ACROSS AMERICA

"Hell of a good read! Wooldridge brings out the best in anyone over 60 who loves bicycling. He inspires readers with a certain elegance of word and deed. I loved his quotes and essays from other riders who love bicycling to the core of their being. Beyond that, he spins a hell of a tale with his buddies and their incredible moments along the Northern Tier of America. No matter if you're 21 or 81, you'll love this adventure from a physical, mental and spiritual standpoint. Just get out there onto the highway for your own bicycle adventure!" James Cochran

"This tale might be the bicycle version of the famous book, **Zen and the Art of Motorcycle Maintenance.** The author delves into the energy of the ride from an old man's perspective. Not only that, he waxes poetic from other travelers like John Steinbeck's **Travels with Charlie.** What I liked is his story telling of "epic moments" from other rides that kept me on, what he calls, "the edge of wonder" while riding his bike. If you ride a bicycle and dream of world travel, you're going to love this book. If you don't love riding a bicycle or world travel, Wooldridge takes you for one hell of a ride while sitting in your easy chair." Scott Hamilton

"I've read many travel books over the years. As a woman, I can say this book grabbed my heart. I love the courage of men. Their courage gives me more courage. I couldn't put it down. I felt like I was riding with this bunch of old coots. Amazingly, they laughed, joked and sang songs around the campfire like they were a bunch of young guys. In fact, other than their gray beards and bald heads, they acted like a bunch of young bucks. It was nice to see that you can outrun "old age" by pedaling your bike faster. Great read for anyone who loves adventure travel." Ann Johnson

"Wooldridge brings stories of his "epic moments" to life in this book. As a man who has bicycled across six continents, he tells some humdingers. At the same time, he adds more epic moments to his life with the ones that occurred on this ride across America. How do you survive a 260,000-acre wildfire in Montana? Or, what about a trifecta moment to see Niagara Falls, rainbows over the falls and an eclipse of the sun? I loved his description of bicycling the Lewis & Clark Trail through the Columbia River Gorge. I felt like I was riding along with his buddies. And his Irish friend who played guitar during the entire trip, what a treat to sing along with them around the campfire. I could smell the smoke and 'see' the stars overhead. Great book!" Hank Curtis

"In this high-speed world, it's nice to slow down to what Wooldridge calls "The Pleasure Pace." Yeah, 12 miles per hour gives you a chance to enjoy every mile of the journey. Wooldridge's compelling prose captured my imagination. I really felt like I was pedaling along with him and his friends. At my tender age of 30, I hope to be living such grand adventures when I reach his age. I liked his inspiring quotes at the head of each chapter. He covers so much ground with such grace and elegance." Anna Lynn

"You like to ride a bike? You ever thought about riding across a continent? Well, you gotta' read this book. It splashes across your mind like a sunny day with raindrops that make you feel good. You can't help but follow Wooldridge's lead and do it yourself. I don't care if you're 30, 40, 50, 60, 70 or 80; you can ride your bicycle across America or the world. Wooldridge even provides you two fantastic chapters that show you which bike to buy, how to outfit yourself and pack lists that you can use to ride in America or around the world. This is the best damned book on bicycle adventure I've ever read." Roger McClendon

"A girlfriend of mine told me to read this book. Since I love bicycling and I belong to a club in Denver, I got a copy. Loved it! I felt my thighs pumping up and down on every page. I felt like I was a part of this journey. That guitar player Gerry caught my attention with his songs by Willie Nelson and Elvis Presley. Lots of funny stuff in this book. I will never forget the coyote chasing the jack rabbit or that hawk taking a rattlesnake at sunset. Totally incredible!" Jane Carr

"At my advanced age of 75, I'm ready to hop on my bike to travel across America. What convinced me? This book! If a bunch of my fellow senior citizens can ride their bikes across America and have that much fun, well hell, I can do it, too. I want to make a statement near the end of my time on this planet. I am going to bicycle across America. This book will be in my panniers the entire way." George Strucker

"Any baby boomers out there, about 80 million of you, who worked your butts off your whole lives bringing up a family, payed the bills and did what you were supposed to do? It's time for you to live your own dreams. If you love bicycling, this band of old guys knows how to have a good time. But it's more than cycling: the author encourages retirees to follow their dreams by backpacking, skiing, sailing, canoeing, painting, pottery making and just about anything that turns you on to your own life. On this journey, these cycling dudes pedal, sing, camp, joke and they laugh a lot. What did I like best about Wooldridge' tale? He showed me that I can pedal my own bike across the country. This is a hell of a great read. Buy it. Learn from it. Then, go do it yourself. He's got everything you need to know at the back of his book. It'll be the best thing you've done in your life. And, he tells you how to buy an E-bike with electric assist, so your wife and you can enjoy cycling adventures together. You truly will live, as Wooldridge said, 'On the edge of wonder.'" Herman Jackson

"This book brings incredible energy to any reader, male or female, young or old. It's got so much wisdom and inspiration. I couldn't help but feel like I could conquer the world while reading this book. It really delves into living at what the author calls, "high vibrational frequency living." When you create adventures in your life, big or small, short term or long term, you live on that "edge of wonder" that the author speaks about. I didn't realize it until I finished the book. That's why I read it twice to cement his concepts into my mind. Great reading and compelling prose." Harold Morgan

Printed in the United States
By Bookmasters